David Crockett's
Non-Execution Death and Apotheosis at the Alamo March 6, 1836

Also by this author

David Crockett's
Non-Execution Death and Apotheosis at the Alamo March 6, 1836

Phillip Thomas Tucker, Ph.D.

Cover image: *Davy Crockett Eventually Falls to the Ceaseless Mexican Attacks* by Luis Arcas Brauner

ISBN: 978-1-79487-493-0

PublishNation LLC
www.publishnation.net

Table of Contents

Prologue

Much like his politically torn nation that he realized was fragile and internally weak, General Antonio Lopez de Santa Anna, the centralist strongman who rose to power to lead the Republic of Mexico in the early 1830s, faced the greatest challenge of his lengthy military and political career by 1836, because of the complex situation that existed in the northeast corner of the Latino republic in Texas.

Here, in Tejas, or Texas, the Anglo-Celtic colonists had rebelled at Gonzales, Texas, against the authority of Mexico and Santa Anna in early October 1835. But this rebellion evolved into no ordinary people's revolt against Mexico as Santa Anna realized, and quite unlike the one recently raised in 1835 by pro-republican and liberal Mexicans on home soil.

This revolt had erupted at Zacatecas, situated in the State of Zacatecas, which was located in north central Mexico and northwest of Mexico City. Here, the largest militia of any Mexican state posed a serious threat to the centralist government because of its size. Fueled by Santa Anna's abandonment of the liberal 1824 Constitution and the legal reduction of state power, including the size of the state militia, the Zacatecas rebellion had been a liberal revolt, with only a few Anglos who were mostly liberal-minded Europeans unlike in Texas. And Santa Anna crushed the revolt with ease and without mercy. Then, he turned north to quell still another rebellion north of the Río Grande River in Texas, which was the richest state in the Mexican Republic.

Also beginning in 1835 to mirror the unrest in liberal Zacatecas which had long relied on its lucrative silver mines for revenue, the Texas rebellion was something altogether different in regard to the contours and currents of its internal dynamics—the very antithesis of the homespun Zacatecas revolt—by early 1836. The Texas Revolution consisted of almost entirely Anglo-Celtic volunteers who had recently come from the United States. By early 1836, most of these men were recent arrivals to Texas from primarily the slave states of the Deep South.

Therefore, by early 1836, the vast majority of the defenders in Texas were not the long-time residents of the Anglo-Celtic colony of Stephen Fuller Austin, who began the settlement of his colony in the early 1820s. Indeed, most of the residents of Texas remained at home in the east Texas settlements and far from the exposed frontier and the locations of the Texas garrisons at San Antonio de Béxar and Goliad, Texas.

This flood of manpower into Texas from the United States was something new in the history of Mexican revolts because of its massive scale, transforming the Texas revolt on the northern frontier into Santa Anna's and Mexico's worst nightmare and ultimate dilemma for the troubled, money-short republic by early 1836: a flood not of peaceful immigrants from the United States but instead large numbers of armed volunteers from America, and they were especially eager to fight for Texas and gain their share of thousands of prime acres of fertile land for their military service in the rebellion.

Therefore, by early 1836, the vast majority of Anglo-Celtic fighting men in Texas were not only from the United States but also recent arrivals, including at the Alamo and other garrisons in Texas, especially at Goliad. Here, at Goliad, Georgia-born Colonel James Walker Fannin commanded hundreds of mostly United States volunteers from across the South.

Unlike the Mexican militia—the largest in Mexico--at Zacatecas which had been ruthlessly crushed by Santa Anna in 1835 and as noted, the forces serving the cause of Texas by early 1836 were almost all Anglo-Celts, mostly citizens from the United States. Only a few Tejanos, Mexicans who had

3

been born in Texas, of Captain Juan Nepomuceno Seguín's Tejano cavalry company fought beside the Anglo-Celts, who hailed from a vastly different culture.

Quite simply, Santa Anna's and Mexico's main problem in 1836 in the upcoming bid to reclaim Texas was this massive foreign intervention of armed citizens from the United States, which was providing the invaluable manpower, support, and fuel for the rebellion against Mexico. Consequently, this rebellion was no longer a people's revolt because the revolution's internal dynamics had significantly changed since the fall of 1835.

And this situation of a mostly revolt of United States citizens, who were recent arrivals to Texas, was especially the case by early 1836, when most native Texans, or colonists, deliberately remained out of military service and at home in their east Texas settlements during the winter. Here, as if no war existed at all, they contentedly tended their farms and ranches as usual, especially paying close attention to the lucrative cotton crop, instead of serving in garrisons to the south, including at the Alamo.

Therefore, at this stage of the war, mostly United States volunteers served in the forces of Texas, and this demographic applied to the Alamo garrison by early 1836, and Colonel

James Walker Fannin's large command at Goliad, Texas. Fannin's force was destined to fail miserably to come to the aid of the Alamo, and then the entire command was massacred—more than 400 victims—when the long lines of unarmed prisoners were marched out into the open prairie on Palm Sunday, March 27, 1836.

At that time and as mentioned, Fannin's troops consisted of hundreds of zealous volunteers recently from the United States, including men from companies like the Red Rovers of Alabama, the Mobile Grays from Mobile, Alabama, and the San Antonio Grays, and the Georgia Battalion.

Consequently, besides the difficult chore of crushing the rebellion in the northeast corner of Mexico, Santa Anna also faced a political crisis of the first magnitude because of the overall weakness and fragility of Mexico, its government, and existing questions about his own dictatorial powers that were still challenged in Mexico City, especially if he met with an unexpected defeat in Texas.

Most of all, therefore, Santa Anna needed to prove the primary source of the most serious existing problem in regard to the rebellion in Texas and the undeniable truth about what was really happening in regard to the Texas Revolution's internal dynamics—massive interference from hundreds of armed citizens of the United States, which supplied manpower, munitions, and even cannon, and not the activities of homegrown, or Tejano, rebels in Texas to enlighten rival politicians and the people of Mexico, the United States, and the world about the fundamental truths of the Texas rebellion.

Such a timely revelation about the most important manpower equation of the Texas Revolution would have allowed Santa Anna to gain the moral high ground in the realm of public opinion around the world. After all, Santa Anna was only attempting to save Texas for Mexico in the face of a sizeable illegal intervention from across the border—the Sabine and Red Rivers--with the United States, which was violating its own Neutrality Laws and basically supporting an illegal war against a country officially at peace with the United States.

General Santa Anna, therefore, was desperately eager for political and military reasons to prove to the world about what was really fueling the revolt against Mexico in Texas, including the Anglo-Celtic garrison at the Alamo. On March 6, 1836, Santa Anna overwhelmed the Alamo in part to gain evidence to make this key political point by proving what was actually happening in Texas—it was no longer a people's rebellion of Texas residents like in 1835--in regard to extensive outside intervention from the United States, which had conveniently ignored its own Neutrality Laws to fuel Santa Anna's and Mexico's sense of outrage to new heights.

In consequence, after overwhelming the small Alamo garrison of mostly recent arrivals from the United States to Texas on the bloody morning of March 6, 1836, Santa Anna sent the captured blue banner of the volunteer company of the New Orleans Greys (two companies of volunteers which had been organized in New Orleans in October 1835) to Mexico City as proof of outside illegal intervention from the United States, after his one-sided victory.

But General Santa Anna had failed in his vital mission of achieving a major propaganda coup when time was short because he had ordered the slaughter of every defender of the Alamo and they were wiped out to the last man. Only the blue flag of the New Orleans Greys, the volunteer unit from New Orleans that had been formed in November 1835 in the Crescent City on the mighty Mississippi, was left to the victorious generalissimo as a trophy to be sent back to Mexico City to prove to one and all that the war in Texas was fueled by large numbers of outsiders from the United States, and who were part of the greatest land grab bags in history—the severing of Texas from Mexico.

Carried to the Central Plains of Texas all the way from New Orleans when young men and boys, including Irishmen, from the United States had only dreamed of martial glory and never imagined the extent of the disasters that awaited them in Texas, this lone flag of silk proved insufficient for Santa Anna's propaganda purposes. In the halls of the Mexican Congress, the display of blue banner from the volunteers of New Orleans helped to gain Santa Anna additional political support in Mexico City for the reconquest of Texas and his centralist policies, but this exhibition still was not enough.

In truth, the greatest proof of outside intervention for significant propaganda purposes that Santa Anna could have utilized to profoundly influence world opinion to make his case—and an excellent one—about the illegality and immorality of massive armed intervention from the United States (a secret not yet known to the rest of the western world outside the United States) would have been to have captured the highest profile American of the Alamo garrison.

And this just happened to be the most famous American of his day, and he had been killed with the rest of the Alamo garrison. A former Tennessee Congressman who many Americans had once thought should have recently embarked upon a presidential bid and the most famous frontiersman of his day, David Crockett.

However, Santa Anna missed his golden opportunity to have gained this famous prisoner on Sunday March 6, 1836 for endless propaganda purposes that would have served him and Mexico extremely well on the world stage and in the realm of public opinion (even in the United States critics, especially abolitionists, charged that the Texas revolt was nothing more than a conspiracy to save and then spread slavery in the future) in regard to a revolution that had been only possible with massive support of funds, weapons, including cannon, and manpower from the United States.

Santa Anna, a master politician above all else and a consummate Machiavellian, missed his golden opportunity to capitalize on nabbing the one American of the Alamo garrison who was a living legend in his own time. Instead, Santa Anna wasted his great opportunity when he decided that the entire garrison should be wiped out to the last man. At that time in the beginning of the Alamo siege and for some time thereafter, Santa Anna had no idea that Crockett was a garrison member, and the famous Tennessean's actions during the siege verified as much.

Then, incredibly, not long after the Alamo's fall, the spread of camp rumors, including from Mexican prisoners who had been captured at San Jacinto on April 21, 1836, swirled that Crockett had been captured and executed on Santa Anna's orders, when his identity was alleged known by the Mexicans.

If this had been the case, then how could Santa Anna have been possibly guilty of committing one of the greatest political mistakes of his career, when his fame was that of a master politician and shrewd propagandist? But was this actually the case, despite Mexican rumors that mentioned Crockett's execution on Santa Anna's direct orders not long after the battle? How did such rumors spread in the first place and where did they originate and why?

After this miserable defeat on the flat coastal plain at San Jacinto which guaranteed the loss of Texas forever to the Mexican nation, Santa Anna's men had turned against their leader. After all, Santa Anna had become the architect of the greatest defeat in Mexican history and then virtually giving away of Texas by treaty to save his life, after the autocratic generalissimo had been captured at San Jacinto.

Quite simply, his former followers, especially the well-educated aristocrats of the Mexican officer corps, had turned against the now thoroughly humbled Santa Anna—he had not been popular with the army's officer corps from the beginning because of his stern, autocratic ways--to save their own lives, as they feared, while prisoners of the victorious Texans on Galveston Island, after San Jacinto.

Mexican officers, therefore, enthusiastically presented tales and common gossip about their pompous leader, who had met his "Waterloo" at San Jacinto, to their captors in the most negative light, which was exactly what the Texans wanted to hear because of the unnecessary slaughter at the Alamo and even to justify their own stealing of Texas. Therefore, they eagerly spread the story—part of camp gossip--of the killing of a handful of Alamo prisoners, including Crockett, not long after the battle had ended.

There is no doubt that some garrison members, a mere handful of men, were in fact captured in the darkened buildings, such as in the low barracks along the south wall, and church after the battle, because this fact has never been in doubt because of existing evidence, and it has been well-documented from a variety of Mexican sources.

But contrary to the persistent rumors and tales that revealed the extent of Santa Anna's cruelty in having ordered the killing of a handful of prisoners after the battle ended, Crockett was not one of these unfortunate men, although it has been long assumed that he was one of these captives, which was simply not the case.

Instead of having been captured and executed on Santa Anna's orders as alleged by the rumors (first Mexican camp rumors and then printed stories in United States newspapers based on those rumors that then later appeared in Mexican accounts, including books) during the summer of 1836, Crockett had been killed in the fighting at the Alamo at age 49 in defense of a new land that had been claimed by the Anglo-Celtic colonists and the United States Volunteers as their own.

From the best available and most reliable primary evidence that emerged about what happened on March 6 from surviving noncombatants, Crockett was not executed in the opinion of this current historian, because of the extent of so many problems, including the lack of provenance, that exists in Mexican accounts, which are dubious and highly-questionable, because they were not written at the time and actually penned long after the battle.

Like no other event in recent memory to an entire generation of Americans, a deep shock and disbelief swept the United States when the news was learned about the slaughter of the Alamo garrison, including Crockett, during the month of March 1836. The stunning news had spread like wildfire that a battle had been fought in faraway Texas near San Antonio de Béxar, and the entire garrison of Texas revolutionaries had been put to death on Santa Anna's orders by way of an arrogant whim in his determination to provide a forceful example to others about the high cost of rebelling against Mexico.

Therefore, from the beginning, Santa Anna wisely kept his political priories foremost because he was most of all a savvy politician, even in regard to wiping out the Alamo garrison to the last man to set a psychological and political example to other rebels, especially American citizens across the United States. So why not capture an American prisoner—not only a well-known but a famous United States citizen--from east of the Sabine River at the Alamo to improve his political position and image on the world stage?

Of course, David Crockett, a national figure well-known to the public, would have been the ideal captive for Santa Anna to have made his moral and political case to the world in regard to the true nature of the Texas Revolution by 1836.

A Strange Destiny Calls

Fate itself had seemingly drawn Crockett to Texas. Crockett had only recently departed Washington, D.C., in defeat during his final bid in the summer of 1835 to win another term in

Congress. He left the nation's capital in absolute disgust with the dirty dealing of insider politics and self-serving politicians not only in the nation's capital, but also in his home state of Tennessee.

Thanks to powerful politics and political tricks from the powerful President Andrew Jackson political machine that were highly-effective, Crockett had been voted out of office by his own people of West Tennessee in August 1835: less than two months before the Texas Revolution erupted to alter Crockett's fate forever like his political defeat. Clearly, Crockett was on a major losing streak that only continued in Texas as if destiny had ordained it, and there was nothing that he could do to change his fate.

For ample good reason, Crockett had turned quite cynical because of the sudden humiliating end of what had once been a promising political career—basically a common man of the frontier people and a poor man's Andy Jackson—until he became his own man by boldly proclaimed his political and personal independence by siding against the day's most powerful political machine. In the end because of a cruel twist of fate, Crockett's fierce sense of independence and loyalty to the common man cost him a political career and eventually his own life in Texas when far from his West Tennessee home, which was in keeping with his national image as a frontier hero.

Therefore, Crockett was thoroughly sick of the United States, including Tennessee because he felt betrayed by his own people, after his political career came crashing down so suddenly around him. In regard to the United States and its crass and cynical politics dominated by excessive lying, deliberate perversions of the truth, and smear campaigns of the most ugly nature, Crockett had made good on his vow that if voted out of office in Congress, then his constituents could "go to hell, and I would go to Texas."

In his disillusionment only a short time after his decisive political defeat in the summer, Crockett and a small party departed West Tennessee on Sunday November 1, 1835. Riding south also made sense to Crockett at this time because a harsh Tennessee winter was on the way, and he followed the V-shaped flocks of Canadian Geese heading south as since from time immemorial. In a letter, Crockett emphasized how he was determined "to explore the Texes (sic) well before I return" to West Tennessee in 1836.

As never before, the bountiful and beautiful land called Tejas, or Texas, beckoned the ex-Congressman with endless new possibilities of a grandiose nature. He was eager to make a fresh start in life, and this all-consuming goal meant first exploring the lush Red River country that was situated along the Texas-Louisiana border at a time, when the temperatures were warm and the sun bright in wintertime unlike in West Tennessee.

When he departed West Tennessee in high spirits, Crockett had embarked upon nothing more than an exploration and hunting trip just south of the Red River. And, of course, he certainly had no plans to getting involved in a risky people's revolution on Texas soil and especially one in which he might be killed far from home and family.

For the disillusioned Crockett and although he still planned to return to West Tennessee, this journey so far southwestward was a one-way trip of no return. More than 850 miles from his West Tennessee home, he was destined to meet an unkind fate and die at the hands of Mexican forces at, of all places, at an old Franciscan mission, where Catholicism had been long worshiped by the Tejano people, or Mexicans who had been born in Texas.

Here, just outside the Tejano town of San Antonio de Béxar located west of the San Antonio River, whose clear waters flowed south from the timbered, well-watered hill country of Edwards Plateau just to the north, Crockett was fated to be killed in battle, dying along with the rest of the small Alamo garrison.

Therefore, in the end, Crockett never lived to see his fiftieth birthday on August 16, 1836. As a cruel fate would have it, Crockett's political career and dream of beginning a new life as a gentleman farmer and the proud owner of hundreds of acres in the fertile Red River country—which he viewed as an unspoiled Eden—of east Texas came to a tragic conclusion even before it had begun.

The shocking news that Crockett, who had been one of the nation's foremost American heroes of his day and certainly the most popular stereotypical frontiersman of the nineteenth century, had been killed at the Alamo stunned the nation primarily because he was a national figure of immense popularity across the breath of the United States.

But there were conflicting reports about how Crockett died on that awful early March morning when no mercy had ruled the day because of Santa Anna's harsh orders. Most Americans could not believe the shocking news of the death of one of their own idols and heroes in far-away Texas, especially at the hands of Mexicans, who they had long deemed as inferior in every way. In this context, Crockett was also a racial hero to an entire generation of Americans because he was widely seen as representing the most ennobling and sterling traits of the American character.

However, at least one man was not surprised or stunned in the least by the disturbing news coming from Texas about Crockett's tragic demise in battle, which had swept across the nation like wildfire. Born in North Carolina and a man of means who possessed a fine University of Pennsylvania education, Dr. Isaac N. Jones was a skilled physician in a remote corner of the country near the Texas border. He owned an excellent plantation, including slaves, on the Red River at Lost Prairie, Arkansas Territory.

Unlike most Americans, Jones had actually met Crockett and took a close measure of this remarkable common man "from the cane" brakes of West Tennessee. This opportunity came after the former Tennessee Congressman and a small part group of Tennessee friends, Lindsey K. Tinkle, and two family members, William Patton (nephew) and Abner Burgin (brother-in-law), had ridden from their homes in Weakley County, West Tennessee, homes in early November 1835.

In high spirits and eager to see the picturesque Red River country, they had only recently trekked the town of Little Rock, Arkansas Territory. Then, Crockett and his small party then rode through the small community of Lost Prairie, founded in 1816 and located in the far southwestern tip of the Arkansas Territory in today's Miller County, Arkansas, during their long journey to Texas.

Along the Red River that flowed southeast as part of the Mississippi River Basin and amid a picturesque countryside full of game and rich soil, this party of friends and relatives stopped at the stately residence of the prosperous Arkansas planter and physician. Here, Crockett requested to spend the night, which was a customary request from weary travelers, who had long benefitted from Southern hospitality and generosity.

Of course, Dr. Jones gladly accommodated, and invited them to join him and his family at the dinner table and to spend the night in extra bedrooms of his large houses. After all, Crockett was nothing less than a revered celebrity to Americans across the land at this time, and Dr. Jones felt honored by the visitation.

The next day, Crockett and the physician, an admirer of the popular frontiersman like so many other Americans, spent time together on the sizeable Jones' plantation along the Red River, which had become prosperous from the growing of cotton and slave labor, when cotton was king. At this point, the Red River, wide, majestic, and distinguished by a swirling current, was reddish in color from the red clay topsoil that had been washed down by floods and rains.

Short of funds, Crockett traded his gold watch, inscribed with his name and which had been presented to him by the young Whig politicians of Philadelphia, Pennsylvania, with one owned of the good doctor. Since Crockett stated that his watch's value was $30 higher than the value of Jones' watch in his humble estimation, the physician than paid Crockett, who was already short on funds, the $30.00 difference. A timely trade, this amount provided much needed money for the continuation of Crockett's long journey to Texas.

When Dr. Jones learned of Crockett's death on that tragic morning at the Alamo, he wrote to the Tennessean's wife, Elizabeth Patton Crockett. Quite a remarkable woman in her own right and the pillar of strength that had long held the family together in her husband's long absences, Elizabeth was Crockett's long-suffering and capable second wife.

She had long skillfully managed the farm, landholdings, and other family businesses during her husband's lengthy absences from home and largely financed his political campaigns for Congress: one forgotten secret of a raw frontiersman's success on the national stage.

In his letter to Elizabeth, Dr. Jones explained the situation of having met her husband at his home in Lost Prairie, Arkansas Territory. And in a kind gesture, he returned Crockett's watch to the ever-faithful Elizabeth—ironically, in an eloquent missive that was quite likely the first news that she had received of her husband's death weeks before, while she was living in a remote section of Weakley County, West Tennessee.

But most important, Dr. Jones presented a memorable patriotic tribute about Crockett's death at that Alamo from what he had read in the most reliable first-person accounts that had been widely published in the nation's newspapers, and one that was right on-target about this remarkable man who had recently met and greatly admired: "His military career was short. But though I deeply lament his death, I cannot restrain my American smile at the recollection of the fact that he died as a United States soldier should die, covered with his slain enemy."

Significantly, Dr. Jones' words were no exaggeration or hyperbole about Crockett's untimely death far from home and family. He had revealed what actually happened to the former Congressman at the Alamo that contradicted the gossip and rumors of his alleged capture and execution, revealing the true manner of his death that had been derived in the best and most dependable primary sources—the accounts of noncombatant survivors, who described in detail what they had seen on March 6 at the Alamo.

But the fundamental truth about the manner of Crockett's final demise at the Alamo has been grossly distorted in recent years as if to garner sensationalism, and nothing has achieved more in changing the traditional perspective of Crockett's heroic death than the so-called diary—actually not even a journal but a postwar memoir which will hereafter be referred to as a memoir—of José Enrique de la Peña.

Entitled *With Santa Anna in Texas, A Personal Narrative of the Revolution*, this manuscript was first published in 1975 by the Texas A&M Press, after it was translated from Spanish to English for the first time by Carmen Perry, who had been born in Mexico. At this time, she was serving capably as the acting director of the Daughters of the Republic of Texas. All in all, Perry was well-qualified for the job of creating the first English version of the de la Peña memoir.

Lieutenant Colonel de la Peña was a member of Santa Anna's Army of Operations during the 1836 Texas Campaign. To now appears that either he, or someone else, included a paragraph about how Crockett was captured and executed in this memoir that was written and composed during a period of several years after the battle at some an undisclosed place in Mexico.

It has been very clear upon close inspection that this alleged diary is not a diary at all but a postwar memoir, which is a significant difference for a variety of reasons: a fact that actually comes close to removing it from the realm of solid and authentic primary evidence. As mentioned, this manuscript is not even a journal. All in all and as noted, the de la Peña manuscript is nothing more than a postwar memoir—a series of Texas Revolutionary War manuscripts written after the war from the writer's vigorous effort to enlarge the original war diary, including from other sources, including period newspapers. All of this material, including postwar sources, was incorporated into a journal that had been based on a wartime diary of Santa Anna's 1836 Texas Campaign.

The real de la Peña diary—allegedly upon which everything written has been based and the true primary source—has never been found or is even known to exist at all to this day. In fact, no one has even seen the war diary of the lieutenant colonel, and no one knows the original source and location of the de la Peña manuscript from 1840 to 1955, except that it came somewhere from the depths of Mexico.

Born in Jalisco, Mexico, in 1800, de la Peña served as a critically-thinking and promising lieutenant colonel in Santa Anna's Army that marched with confidence into Texas to crush the Anglo-Celtic revolt in early 1836. Most troubling was the fact that this memoir suddenly appeared out of thin air in Mexico City, Mexico, in 1955 and, most suspiciously, at the height of the Crockett craze, fueled by Disney, that swept the "Baby Boom" generation across the United States during the early years of the Cold War. Quite simply to this day, no one has any idea or clue where this manuscript was located in Mexico for more than a century.

This book was first published in Mexico City, Mexico, in 1955 by Jesús Sánchez García—a self-published book that was not authenticated by any legitimate publisher, editor, or scholar, who would have been immediately troubled by the complete lack of provenance of the manuscript and other inherent problems with the postwar memoir. Was it authentic or fake? No one even asked this key question or sufficiently cared before the book was published.

Not even Mexican experts and scholars raised this all-important question before García self-published the de la Peña memoir—it literally emerged out of thin air with no background, history, or past. Worst of all, García never revealed the source of the manuscript and how it ultimately came into his eager hands for self-publication in the first place. This central mystery about the manuscript's provenance exists to this day, but this has been mostly overlooked by American historians and scholars, as if no problems existed at all. However, the astonishing lack of provenance still offers a serious problem about the unknown source of the memoir.

Even more alarming, the de la Peña memoir, which was written by a young lieutenant colonel who served in Santa Anna's contingent of his crack engineers, or sappers, was accepted then and to this day, even in Texas, as authentic, despite the lack of provenance and different handwriting found in a manuscript that was penned over a lengthy period of time and years after the war's end.

So by any measure and as noted, this manuscript is certainly not a traditional diary or journal as alleged, but a postwar memoir, with the manuscript having grown in length over the years during an extensive rewriting process. And de la Peña's own handwriting has never been authenticated by scholars, experts, and historians, although the paper of the journal has been authenticated as from the correct period of time (1825 to 1832) and produced by a legitimate company in Lisbon,

Portugal, but these two are vastly different considerations and certainly not one in the same.

Indeed, the exact dating of the paper and the maker are less important than exactly when the ink from a quill pen was placed on the papers of the manuscript. After all and as proven often to have been the case, a savvy forger could have acquired authentic period paper and written his account (a single paragraph) of Crockett's alleged execution death on authentic de la Peña journal paper in a short narrative that was partly derived from newspaper accounts, when all kinds of rumors circulated, including about the alleged execution of Crockett on Santa Anna's orders.

As noted, the García book of the de la Peña memoir was then translated into English for the first time and edited by Carmen Perry and published by the Texas A&M University Press in 1975 without the usual provenance, as in the case of other historical manuscripts to determine if the manuscript was authentic or forged. Because of García's self-publication in Mexico City when there was no scrutiny of any kind or legitimate questions asked about the manuscript's mysterious origins, the absence of the all-important provenance, and the manuscript's entirely unknown history before García's sent it to a Mexican press for publication in 1955, the Texas A&M

University Press relied upon a sizeable leap of faith in even publishing the book in 1975.

Nevertheless, this manuscript is actually a journal—based on a war diary—that the evolved into a postwar memoir during years of rewriting, but it is an authentic document. But what is more open to question is the brief words in a single paragraph about Crockett's alleged death by execution at the hands of Santa Anna's men and upon the generalissimo's express orders inside the Alamo compound after the battle, because it was written during the postwar period, when tales of Crockett's execution had become rumor and had been previously published in United States newspapers.

Of course, we definitely do know for a fact that de la Peña had a war diary—very obvious when reading the details found in the manuscript--that he enlarged into a sizeable memoir for at least three years after the Texas Revolution. During this period of writing and rewriting, de la Peña might well have incorporated the accounts in United States newspapers. These stories first appeared in the summer of 1836 and later, for popular reading in Mexico if translated and reprinted in Spanish, about Crockett's alleged execution that first came from Mexican camp gossip based on exaggeration and not facts, and Mexican oral accounts, including from captured men, who had turned against Santa Anna: the most likely genesis of the alleged Crockett execution story as it appeared in a single paragraph in the lieutenant colonel's memoir that was written after the war.

Although it has been verified that the lieutenant colonel's memoir was written on authentic paper of the period, different handwriting has been ascertained on its pre-Texas Revolution era paper to reveal that more than one author was involved in the writing and rewriting process of the manuscript after the war.

Of course and as mentioned, this situation does not omit the possibility that a modern hand wrote the Crockett execution paragraph on old, authentic paper. Forgers become expert forgers because they carefully obtain the right aged paper upon which to write a historical account to fool the experts and reap a profit from their skill in the art of deception to fool a gullible public, including historians who had long fallen victim like everyone else.

In his memoir in what is more troubling than the alleged execution of the famous Tennessean, de la Peña even denies that Crockett was a soldier of Texas. The de la Peña memoir emphasized that "naturalist David Crockett . . . who had undertaken to explore the country and who, finding himself in

Béxar at the very moment of surprise [on February 23], had taken refuge in the Alamo, fearing that his status as a foreigner might not be respected."

Of course, this explanation is simply not true because Crockett had enlisted in east Texas, and he had signed an oath of allegiance to Texas to become a private in the Texas Army in mid-January 1836. And, of course, he was a member of the company commanded by Captain William B. Harrison's Tennessee Mounted Volunteers, when stationed at the Alamo. All of these facts are well-known and well-documented.

Even more, some Mexican accounts emphasized that Crockett, who was described as wearing buckskins and a distinctive cap of fur, was a prominent fighter and crack marksman, who was often seen firing effectively from the Alamo's walls and demonstrated a high level of inspired leadership during the siege.

However, the besieging Mexicans did not know that Crockett was a member of the garrison as long alleged. Primary evidence, including Lieutenant Colonel William Barret Travis' own words that praised Crockett's leadership abilities during the siege, exists about the Tennessean's inspired role in defending the Alamo by distinguished acts before the final attack.

But even more, the first report received by Texas forces about the Alamo disaster had failed to mention an alleged Crockett execution. Two members of Captain Juan Nepomuceno Seguín's cavalry company of Tejanos, who fought for the cause of Texas with distinction, brought the first news of the Alamo's fall to the east. They presented a surprisingly detailed and accurate report about the grim news of the Alamo's fall and details about the slaughter of the garrison to General Sam Houston at Gonzales, Texas, on April 11, 1836.

These two Tejano cavalrymen, Andres Barcena and Anselma Bergeras, had gained detailed information in San Antonio from Tejanos and Santa Anna's soldados, who had fought at the Alamo, including how the most prominent defenders died on that fateful morning. This first-hand information even included how the Alamo commander, Lieutenant Colonel William Barret Travis, had died by committing suicide—shocking information that General Houston, nevertheless, dutifully passed along with other leading Texas revolutionaries, both military and civilian, because this was the first detailed and accurate news of the Alamo's fall.

But despite all of the intimate details about the fate of the Alamo garrison and the battle that they revealed to Houston on March 11, Barcena and Bergeras never mentioned anything about the alleged capture of Crockett and his alleged execution, as later spread by rumor that appeared in United States newspapers. If Crockett had been executed after the battle as alleged, then these two Tejanos certainly would have learned as much and then passed along the word to General Houston like in the case of Travis' death, because the mayor of San Antonio de Bexar had identified Crockett's body to Santa Anna. But they did not.

Indeed, the two Tejanos remained perfectly silent about any executions at the Alamo, including Crockett, because they had failed to hear anything about them. Consequently, there was no mention by the two cavalrymen at all of Crockett's fate other than that fact that he was killed with the other garrison members.

In fact, no Mexican Army report, including by Santa Anna, written on March 6, 1836 mentioned anything about Crockett's alleged execution just like in regard to the accurate information that was forthcoming to General Houston from the two Tejanos of Captain Seguín's cavalry command on March 11: an omission that verified the truth of the actual situation before the rumors and camp gossip--with no basis—about Crockett's alleged suicide death had spread.

Likewise, Anglo-Celtic civilian survivors of the battle, including the wife of Captain Almeron Dickinson, Tennessee-born Susanna Wilkerson Dickinson, and Travis' slave Joe, said nothing about Crockett's alleged execution, and their accounts are not only reliable but also accurate about what happened. In fact, their first-person accounts have revealed that Crockett was killed—they did not see his death but saw his slain body after the fighting concluded--with his men of Captain Harrison's Tennessee Company near the church and the low palisade that linked the southwest corner of the Alamo church to the buildings of the low barracks (the south wall).

Both Joe and Susanna Dickinson emphasized that Crockett and his fellow Tennesseans were surrounded by fallen Mexicans—a verified Crockett battle death, where he stood and fought for some time, from eyewitnesses as opposed to having been allegedly executed at another location in the open plaza, where Santa Anna was located, or perhaps even called his temporary headquarters, as indicated by some Mexican accounts.

If Crockett had been killed after the battle, then the non-combatant survivors would have seen the execution. But, as mentioned, neither Joe or Susanna said anything about Crockett's execution because there simply was none as alleged by Mexican sources, and their repeated testimony and accounts have revealed as much.

Joe told of Travis' death in defending the north all but he failed to describe Crockett's death, because he never saw it since the popular Tennessean fell in battle near the low palisade and the front of the church, while Joe had been near the opposite end of the sprawling compound at the north wall, when his master was killed at the 3-gun battery. Joe then retired into the Alamo compound to seek shelter like other defenders when the north wall was breached.

Joe, still a slave of the Travis estate after the Alamo's fall, presented more oral accounts of the battle, including Travis' death, and more accurate details than another survivor on the Texas side. And Joe made not a single mention of Crockett's alleged execution death. All of his words indicated that Crockett died in a distinct battle setting, where he fought to the bitter end as evident from the number of Mexican dead around him.

Again, if anyone would have seen Crockett's alleged execution death, then it would have been Joe and Susanna because they were taken out into in the open plaza of the

Alamo compound, where the alleged execution supposedly occurred not long after the firing ended. Because both Joe and Susanna were hidden inside rooms in the church during the battle, they could <u>not</u> have seen Crockett's death in battle, but they <u>would have seen</u> his allegedly death by execution after the battle if that had been the case, after they were led out into the open plaza.

In the end, the alleged Crockett execution was never mentioned by any of these Alamo noncombatant survivors who would have not only seen, but also would have heard about the execution not long after the battle ended. However, such anti-Crockett execution facts, which have contradicted the Mexican execution accounts, have been negated and forgotten partly because of the sudden excitement over the appearance of the de la Peña memoir as self-published by Mr. Garza, a shadowy, mysterious figure to say the least, in Mexico City 1955 without any kind of provenance whatsoever.

Even more, the Mexican accounts, including anonymous ones and those without provenance that seemed entirely based on camp gossip in which rumors of all kinds ran wild, of Crockett's alleged execution death contain a host of errors and contradictions, including even the place of execution, the precise scenario of Crockett's post-battle demise, who [Santa

Anna's staff officers or enlisted men] exactly committed the actual killing, and the exact manner of execution, to an extremely wide degree, which has reduced the credibility of the Mexican accounts, including the de la Peña memoir, which has seem gossipy as best.

However, the fundamental players and personalities, including Mexican officers, such as Major General Manuel Fernándo Castrillón who was known for his compassion and took a few prisoners and then attempted to have them spared in opposition to orders, in the execution from Santa Anna's direct orders have remained basically the same: suspiciously, this situation seems as if one single account had actually been the original source of the later Mexican accounts, including the de la Peña memoir.

Like Santa Anna, Castrillón knew nothing of Crockett's presence—a new arrival and unexpected volunteer--at the Alamo during the siege and also evidently afterwards. As a cruel fate would have it, the only Mexico general who attempted to save lives at the Alamo was fated to be shown no mercy and killed at San Jacinto by Houston's enraged soldiers.

Consequently, in summary, the details of these Mexican soldado accounts, around a half dozen that were not written on March 6 or immediately thereafter, and American newspapers rumors of Crockett's alleged execution were seemingly incorporated into the de la Peña manuscript at a later date in a single paragraph, which has indicated that the lieutenant colonel was not actually an eyewitness to the event.

From all of the best available evidence and given the special circumstances in regard to questions and issues that still exist about the legitimacy of the José Enrique de la Peña memoir, although he served in the elite battalion known as the Zapadores, or Sapper, Battalion, and other dubious Mexican sources in general, it is the opinion of this current author that Crockett never surrendered as alleged. Quite simply, he fought to the last with his fellow Tennesseans, which was more accurately revealed by the words of Joe and Susannah.

And given the best and most reliable primary evidence, he was certainly not executed, especially as depicted in the over-the-top, if not grotesque, manner in the 2004 John Lee Hancock film *The Alamo*. Instead, he simply died fighting with other garrison members, especially the men of Captain William B. Harrison's Tennessee Mounted Volunteers, and he fell victim to attackers in the heat of battle: the common view of Crockett's demise by Alamo civilian survivors, especially Joe but also Susanna Dickinson, at the time, and the absence of any alleged execution in the first report on March 11, 1836 to

General Houston by Seguín's Tejano cavalrymen in the service of Texas.

For whatever reason, Hancock's lavishly embellished and fanciful version of Crockett's alleged execution death in the open plaza of the Alamo compound was merely the creation of the screenwriter's vivid imagination, especially the imaginary exchange of dialogue between Santa Anna and a tightly-bound Crockett, who was portrayed on his knees in the ultimate position of submission.

Even more, Hancock presented the impossible, if not ridiculous, scenario that Crockett was very well well-known among the peasant troops of Santa Anna's Army, including enlisted men, and that they even revered the Crockett legend to a degree in Santa Anna's Army of Operations.

In truth, the generalissimo knew nothing about the man who had been captured and was bound before him by rope and on his knees in this imaginary scenario of the screenwriter: an incredible stretch of imagination and especially in regard to any possibility of the alleged widespread admiration for Crockett among the enemy, who were some of the most xenophobic people in North America, especially the mostly illiterate peasants of the Mexican Army, who possessed with little, if any, interest in the United States and its citizens.

Quite simply, the mostly illiterate common soldiers of Santa Anna's Army and even well-educated Mexican officers knew nothing about Crockett, his reputation, or his appearance on March 6. As noted, Santa Anna knew nothing about Crockett's presence until he was shown the bodies of the Alamo's leaders by the mayor, Ruiz, of San Antonio de Béxar.

Nevertheless, the Hancock film created the fantasy that the Crockett legend was so great that it had somehow spread and extended deep into Mexico, to become well-known to the average soldados in Santa Anna's Army, which, of course, was an utter impossibility. Clearly, this was an assumption about 1836 from a modern viewpoint that had nothing to do with the historical facts and realities.

Of course, there is no historical evidence of such a situation as depicted by Hancock, which is a rather odd inclusion in the film given that the film's strength lay in its reliance upon accuracy in historical detail and facts, as long emphasized by the filmmakers for promotional and sales purposes. Therefore, Hancock based his Crockett execution scenario on not only very little evidence, but also on contradictory and highly questionable Mexican sources that came to light after the war had ended—again no primary documentation from Mexican sources immediately after the battle, especially on March 6 in the form of a diary, letter, or journal, which would have been undisputable.

All in all, Hancock's overly-dramatic fictional version of Crockett's alleged execution, of course, was only the creation from the over-imaginative mind of a screenplay writer, who penned the alleged dialogue between the victim and Santa Anna of a most fantastic nature, which had which had no basis in fact. What the film's execution portrayal represented was the height of political correctness and how far America has evolved in its most unheroic and irreligious age.

Indeed, the 2004 version of Crockett's alleged execution closely resembled the ridiculous realm of the cartoonish, which proved insulting to Crockett's historical memory, and grotesque on multiple levels. And it was evidently created in order to enhance sales from movie goers by way of sparking controversary. All in all, the much-embellished story of Crockett's alleged execution has become a modern and politically correct tale in the fictional tradition of the *Crockett Almanacs* and just as incredible.

If this not-so-clever plan for promotional purposes through sensationalism of Crockett's alleged execution death was the case, then it backfired miserably at the box office because Hancock's *The Alamo* was a commercial disaster.

Clearly and by any measure, filmmakers and historians have given too much credence to the brief entry (a single paragraph) of the alleged Crockett execution in the de la Peña memoir—perhaps fabricated in Mexico by a forger for the express purpose of reaping a greater financial reward from the sale of the de la Peña manuscript (a strategy that certainly succeeded in the United States, especially in Texas where it eventually was deemed without question to have been an authentic historic document and garnered a high price--$350,000 when purchased by two Texans in 1998), which had suddenly emerged out of thin air in Mexico City in 1955—at the height of the Crockett craze in America in what was much more than an astonishing coincidence of the first order.

Quite simply, Hancock's distorted, if not somewhat perverse focus, on presenting the most controversial aspect of the Alamo's story in such vivid, embellished detail in regard to Crockett's execution death was clearly the zenith—reached in 2004—of the long-going mythmaking about the Alamo's story and the apex of the excesses of political correctness in transforming an American hero's story into something that was unheroic, if not tawdry, in the tradition of political correctness.

Significantly and as noted, the de la Peña memoir was published in 1975, when Saigon, the capital of South Vietnam, fell to the victorious forces of the North Vietnamese Army and the Viet Cong. This time period witnessed the very peak of American defeatism and cynicism about itself and the world in general, because of the disastrous course of events and the absolute folly of the Vietnam War that resulted in the American nation's own loss of innocence that vanished in the tropical jungles and rice paddies of Southeast Asia.

Here, in defiance of the time-honored axiom of the wise need to avoid land wars in Asia at all costs, America betrayed herself and its lofty egalitarian principles in South Vietnam, allowing its one-time ally to fall to the invaders from the north, after cutting off all support and aid—a crass abandonment by the United States Congress and the American nation of a faithful ally—that resulted in one of its greatest humiliation in the nation's history.

Therefore, the political climate and situation, both at home and aboard, was ripe for the distorted presentation of the most controversial account of Crockett's death at the Alamo to significantly reduce his lofty status as a genuine American hero in the tradition of political correctness and cynicism, which had become fashionable by this time.

Therefore, the release of de la Peña memoir in 1975, when a disgraced and humiliated America saw the collapse of its ally in South Vietnam, which had been left on its own without any additional United States support (American troops had been earlier withdrawn and financial aid had been cut off by Congress before 1975) to be completely overwhelmed by the North Vietnamese and their Viet Cong allies, was highly suspicious. And in 1955, the Spanish version of the de la Peña journal was first self-published in Mexico City, despite the lack of provenance. Therefore, to raise doubts and suspicious, these two developments occurred the height of the Crockett craze in the United States in 1955 and the low ebb of America's fortunes in Vietnam and international image around the world in 1975.

These rather remarkable coincidences—not once but twice-- in regard to timing was certainly no coincidence. In overall terms, this situation certainly lends more credibility to the belief, as long articulated by historian Bill Groneman, that the account of Crockett's alleged execution was in fact a forgery, or written by someone other than de la Peña, who almost certainly relied on old newspaper accounts about the alleged Crockett execution during the postwar period or later.

In fact, it is the view of this current writer that perhaps nothing has more strongly pointed more to the illegitimacy of the de la Peña memoir than the curious timing—at the lowest point of America's fortunes with the disastrous turn of events in Vietnam and overall image in the world—of the publication of the de la Peña memoir in the United States in 1975, which just happened to have been the lowest ebb of America's fortunes on the international stage.

Since this low point of America's image overseas and around the world, the de la Peña memoir has predictably become accepted today in its entirety in America's most cynical, unheroic, and irreligious age in which traditional values, including what little is left of the decimated nuclear family, have been thoroughly eroded, much like the gross inefficiency of its educational system (the so-called "Dumbing Down of America"), which ranks extremely low compared to other counties, including many Third World nations.

Today, the popularity of the myth of Crockett's death has been in vogue to this day in America's most anti-heroic period in which traditional American heroes have been torn down for decades by liberals and progressives in the name of political correctness in the overall process of unraveling American culture: a cynical environment that paved the way for Hancock's distorted film version in 2004 and the general acceptance of the Crockett execution story, despite the lack of primary evidence that should have been written on March 6 and shortly thereafter, if there had been an actual execution.

All in all, the Mexican accounts of Crockett's dismal fate by an alleged execution have lacked credibility on multiple levels, especially in regard to why and when they were written (all postwar and in almost certainly the case of one account having inspired other similar accounts) and then made public.

Like in regard to Crockett's alleged execution, the 1840 rumor that he had been captured at the Alamo and then sent to labor for years in Mexico's Salinas underground salt mine (sincerely believed by his son John Wesley Crockett, then a Tennessee Congressman, who acted upon the false intelligence by attempting to initiate an official investigation that might have led to an attempted rescue mission, which, of course, would have paid no dividends), where he had allegedly labored as a slave for years, flourished to the point of having gained acceptance by many Americans.

The belief in Crockett's alleged execution on March 6, 1836 has continued to thrive to this day, thanks to the publication of the de la Peña memoir and Hancock's Alamo movie, which packed a considerable one-two punch in the name of political correctness and because of the heavier reliance on Mexican sources.

Ironically, even more than books about the Alamo, Alamo films have been first and last reserve—at least until 2004 with the release of Hancock's film—of the heroic Crockett death in battle. However, generations of American filmmakers, from *The Last Command* (1955) to Wayne's *The Alamo* (1960) had gone entirely too far in excessively glorifying Crockett's death in the most fantastic and dramatic way by portraying him as having embarked upon the heroic mission of blowing up the black powder magazine housed in back room located in the Alamo Church. This situation was certainly not the case, because the powder magazine was never ignited by a defender's flaming torch and no historical evidence of Crockett's alleged mission exists to this day.

In addition, blowing up the garrison's powder reserve in one of the back rooms of the Alamo church was the crucial assignment of Irishman Major Robert Evans. He was truly one of the Alamo's forgotten heroes in part because of his ethnic background from the Emerald Isle.

The handsome major had been born in 1800 in the town of Derry, County Londonderry, Ulster Province, in north Ireland. One of the largest and strongest garrison members and much taller than Crockett, who was only of average size and not the powerful physical giant of the romanticized frontier image and superhero of the *Crockett Almanacs*, the blue-eyed and dark-haired Evans was the chief of ordnance at the Alamo.

He was in charge of the black powder magazine. Like so many of his fellow countrymen from the Green Isle, Evans had migrated to America at age 23 in 1827 in search of a better life and future, eventually settling in New Orleans, Louisiana.

According to all existing accounts, including that of eyewitness Susanna Dickinson, Evans was shot down by Mexican soldados before he could reach the powder magazine and died with a flaming torch in his hand. Here, in a back room of the Alamo church, the brave Derryman from Ulster Province, north Ireland, died a heroic death in attempting to blow-up the powder magazine.

Clearly, according to all historical sources, it was definitely not Crockett, who was killed outside the church (the powder magazine was situated in a rear room inside the church), because it was Evans who had been given this key assignment, when it appeared that all hope was lost and the Alamo was about to fall.

With no evidence at all in the historical record that Crockett had anything at all to do with the blowing up (which was never blown up) of the Alamo's powder magazine like the imaginary scenario of John Wayne's heroic portrayal of Crockett's final moments in the 1960 film *The Alamo* in the most fanciful and unrealistic of all Alamo films, Crockett actually died in battle in rather unspectacular fashion compared to the glorified powder room scenario. Like other garrison members, he died amid the swirl of combat as only a "high private," in his own words. Nevertheless, Crockett died heroically in the Alamo's defense, but not in a superhuman role as long portrayed in Alamo books and films.

Indeed, the mythical Alamo had created the mythical Crockett, which called for the mythical heroic, if not superhuman, effort that resulted in a memorable ending in keeping with the frontiersman's iconic image, such as the blowing up the Alamo's powder magazine, which was simply not the case.

Nevertheless, in the end, Crockett went down fighting in the end with fellow garrison members, and that tragic ending was entirely sufficient to have placed him permanently in the pantheon of American heroes to this day.

In the end, therefore, Dr. Jones of Lost Prairie (no longer an existing town in Arkansas) was entirely correct when he penned with pride to Crockett's widow Elizabeth how: "I cannot restrain my American smile at the recollection of the fact that he died as a United States soldier should die, covered with his slain enemy."

This view of Crockett's heroic demise on March 6, 1836 was supported by the best and most accurate accounts, especially by Joe, the slave of the Alamo's commander William Barret Travis, at the time and not long after the fact than Mexican accounts. As noted, Colonel Almonte's journal made no mention at all about Crockett and any execution on March 6, because he failed to recognize the Tennessean, who he did not know was present, and because it never happened. Otherwise, Almonte would have certainly noted the execution of one of the most famous Americans in his journal.

Significantly and in no uncertain terms, Joe emphasized what he had seen in one of his many oral interviews that he presented for public consumption, stating in no uncertain terms how Crockett and his fellow volunteers from Tennessee "were found lying together, with 21 of the slain enemy around them."

Most important, it is now time that the words of an African American and Alabama-born slave should be accepted and finally believed at face value (today black oral history has gained greater acceptance in the historical community, as in the case of the long-existing Thomas Jefferson and Sally Hemings relationship at Monticello, Virginia) at long last after having been long discounted and ignored for generations by Americans, especially since he was not owned by Crockett to reveal no personal basis in his presentation of what he had seen at the Alamo on March 6, 1836.

Quite simply, Joe provided Americans of the day with reliable, accurate, and detailed accounts of what actually transpired inside the Alamo, including in regard to Crockett's death in battle, because he simply reported what he had seen with his own eyes.

In the end on the cold morning of March 6 while far from his West Tennessee home, Crockett died with his comrades of Captain Harrison's company of Tennessee boys, and his blood-soaked body was found beside the bodies of these men of his home state, after they had defended the low palisade and later a secondary position in the front of the Alamo church, after the Mexicans had poured over the north wall and other points in triumph by this time.

Phillip Thomas Tucker, Ph.D.
Central Florida
November 15, 2019

Introduction

Mythmaking of Crockett's Execution Death

In 2004 and at long last, the lengthy history of Alamo films have almost certainly finally come to an end, after an amazing run of nearly a century. And like in regard to the final Battle of the Alamo, so the last Alamo film, which began with *The Immortal Alamo* in 1911 and *Martyrs of the Alamo* in 1915 by D. W. Griffith, who in the same year also released the infamous silent film *Birth of a Nation,* ended in a cinematic disaster in overall financial terms.

Alamo films, especially in the 1950s, continued to be made with good results all the way to 2004 with John Lee Hancock's 2004 film *The Alamo*, which ended in a box office disaster of the first magnitude. Therefore, almost certainly, there will be no more Alamo films because this fascinating subject has been beaten to death and run its natural course.

Reflective of the era in which they were made, these two Griffith films were filled with the day's common racial stereotypes, one about blacks and the other, of course, about Mexicans. As could be expected, this situation was fortunately not the case with the 2004 Hancock film, which smartly steered clear of complex and unsettling racial issues because of twenty-first century racial priorities and sensibilities of more enlightened audiences and the desire to turn a nice profit at the box office.

A native Texan whose passion for the Alamo was fully evident to one and all in his fine film, Hancock's *The Alamo* revealed his lifelong admiration of the Alamo, which was something that modern audiences, especially younger ones, in the twenty-first century shared no parallel and even less appreciation for the Alamo's story in reverent terms during the twenty-first century, as demonstrated by the fact that the film was the biggest box office failure in film history: no small accomplishment.

But this situation was entirely understandable, because times in America had significantly changed like the nation itself and the heyday of the American public's fascination in the Alamo has long since passed. Quite simply, Americans have moved on and have grown up past the old childish fantasies of the

1950s, fueled by Disney and other Alamo films, and 1960s and the many romantic myths that have had surrounded the Alamo's story to an excessive degree from the beginning.

For nearly a century, what all of these Alamo films have faithfully presented to the public was the traditional story of the Alamo beginning in 1911: the most famous heroic tale of the Texas Revolution in which a small band of freedom fighters courageously defended the Alamo in the name of liberty for all by boldly defying the dictator Santa Anna and dying to the last man on the bloody morning of March 6, 1836. Such selfless heroism of garrison members, including Crockett, in the face of impossible odds and a ruthless foreign dictator have inspired successive generations of Americans, especially youth, for more than 150 years.

In 1955 during the airing of a three-part series that captivated the American nation to demonstrate the power of television over a new generation of youth, Walt Disney released *Davy Crockett at the Alamo*. The most memorable part of this extremely popular film was the final scene, which depicted Crockett engaged in hand-to-hand combat, which, of course, he was destined not to survive.

And in the last frame of the action, he was portrayed as entirely alone and wildly swinging his empty flintlock musket,

"Old Betsey" at his horde of faceless attackers—apparently the last man remaining still alive of the entire garrison—as a tide of Mexicans gradually overwhelmed him before a fade-away to the flapping Texas flag still flying from the Alamo's wall: a popular film device that was neatly employed by Disney to avoid the depiction of Crockett's grisly death that would have shocked young audiences of admirers and to appeal to child consumers of the "Baby Boom" generation.

This famous final scene once from Disney again catapulted Crockett into the realm of patriotic frontier hero at a time when America was in a possible nuclear collision course with the Soviet Union during the early years of the Cold War. At this time of great national uncertainty and America's heightened collective fear about a more threatening world—a nuclear one-- seemed to be represented by the ruthlessness of dictator Santa Anna and his faceless mass of fanatical attackers of a darker hue, America needed a legitimate white hero—a good old White Anglo Saxon Protestant (WASP)--for the masses to worship.

And, of course, it was magic of Disney, the master showman of modern times, who provided still another one in timely fashion to the American public, especially to the "Baby Boom" generation of the post-Second World War period, by dusting off and resurrecting an old nineteenth century frontier hero second to none. It was a brilliant and most lucrative choice.

From the first Alamo film in 1911 (*The Immortal Alamo*) to John Wayne's *The Alamo* in 1960, only a surprisingly few words of preamble and introduction at the beginning of each film by the screenwriters summarized the overall historical setting of 1836 and what was at stake in the simplistic and idealistic terms in both of these Alamo films that spanned nearly a half century: dictatorship versus republicanism, freedom versus slavery.

Of course, this brutal clash of civilizations (Mexican versus Anglo-Celtic) in 1836 on Texas soil provided the ideal propaganda stage for America's showdown with the relentless march of Communism—the modern dictatorial and totalitarian government not of the people—in the Third World during the Cold War, when the United States was the leader of the free world and represented the republican concept of the government by the people. But, in truth, the 1836 showdown at the Alamo was a great deal more complex on multiple levels than as has been commonly portrayed.

The historical Battle of the Alamo was quite the opposite of the alleged epic clash of arms, which seemed to grow in scale and scope with each new film version of the Alamo's story. During an extremely short battle on the cold morning of March 6 because garrison members had been caught by surprise in their sleep at night against a superior number of attackers, the less than 200 defenders never had a chance, and the battle actually more resembled an intense, close-range skirmish than an epic clash of arms in the traditional sense.

Nevertheless, the traditional story of the Alamo, whose defenders were mostly United States citizens and not Texans, became the sainted heroes of not only Texas but also of America, has been based on the creation of a simplistic morality tale of good versus evil. Meanwhile, all of the seemingly endless number of complexities and contradictions of the Texas Revolution and this brief battle fought mostly in the dark on March 6, 1836 were conveniently, if not shamelessly, painted in the most simplistic shades of black and white in books and films to excessively romanticize and glorify the mythical Alamo instead of focusing on the historical facts of the real Alamo.

Significantly, the James Lee Hancock film of 2004 veered sharply away from the traditional narrative of the Alamo's story, which has basically remained the same for more than 175 years except in regard to one fundamental aspect, as if hoping that an added touch of sensationalism might effectively generate interest and increase ticket sales for *The Alamo*.

Despite the lack of solid historical evidence and reliable documentation from primary sources, Hancock's imaginary depiction, which was artificially invented out of thin air from a screenwriter's imagination run wild, focused on the alleged execution death of Crockett, who had long represented and symbolized the western frontier experience in both fact and legend.

In this way, the Texas filmmaker had actually only repeated the longtime rumor of Crockett's alleged execution that extended back to the Mexican camp talk and the gossipy American newspapers of 1836, which stated that the former Tennessee Congressman had been found hiding in a room—either in the church or the low barracks—and was then executed on Santa Anna's direct orders, after the battle had ended: a rumor that was reconfirmed by the single paragraph that appeared in the 1975 publication of the José Enrique de la Peña memoir, entitled *With Santa Anna in Texas, A Personal Narrative of the Revolution* and translated and edited by Carmen Perry.

In 1975, no one seemed to notice or care at the time that the Crockett execution story was an old one, extending all the way back to just after the battle of fought. This single paragraph in the de la Peña memoir about the alleged Crockett execution was basically presented as a new finding at the time, which was simply not the case.

However, Crockett's alleged execution death had never been depicted on film before until 2004, because of the predominate belief that he had gone down fighting fiercely beside other garrison members, especially the men of Captain Harrison's Tennessee company of volunteers: essentially, the traditional Alamo story line since the time of the famous battle. In this regard, Hancock's sensational 2004 depiction was a first of its kind in vividly presenting Crockett's execution. Such a graphic portrayal of Crockett's demise would have been entirely unimaginable in the past, especially without the publication of the Lieutenant Colonel de la Peña memoir in English in 1975.

Evidently, for the combined effect of commercial reasons and shock value, Hancock decided to resurrect this old rumor—now reinforced by the sensationalism of the de la Peña memoir which was hastily deemed legitimate and authentic by the so-called experts sitting in the smug comfort of their ivy towers of their isolated academe worlds, including in Texas--to the fullest to depict one of the most controversary aspects of the Alamo's story: the long-existing rumor that Crockett had survived the battle after having had taken cover in the church or a room in the low barracks along the south wall, and then he either surrendered or was captured, before he was taken out in the open plaza and executed on the direct order of General Antonio Lopez de Santa Anna.

Evidently, in part concerned about generalissimo appearances if he reversed his earlier order of no quarter for the defenders, Santa Anna had directed that no prisoners were to be taken, since the siege's beginning and refused to deviant from that initial decision after the battle. Consequently, a nearby detail of soldados or staff officers, depending on the Mexican account, then allegedly brutally executed Crockett and a few other garrison members on Santa Anna's order.

However, as derived from the best available and most reliable primary evidence that are available, Crockett never did surrender in part because garrison members already knew that they could not surrender in this battle, which was a fight to the death. Indeed, the dark intentions of Santa Anna, the self-styled "Napoleon of the West," and his harsh no quarter order, which had earlier been issued to his obedient men of the Army of Operations, were already well-known to garrison members throughout the siege of the Alamo for more than a week and a half.

Not long after the advance elements of his Army of Operations captured San Antonio de Béxar on February 23, 1836 and just narrowly missed swooping up the garrison before its members escaped east on the double and into the safety of the comforting shelter of the Alamo's high stone and adobe walls, Santa Anna ordered his men to host a large, bright red flag of no quarter at the top of the highest point—the tall bell tower, or steeple, of San Fernándo Catholic Cathedral, which was located on the main plaza of San Antonio de Béxar .

This infamous red flag of no quarter had been easily seen day after day by the men of the Alamo flapping in the winter winds that swept across the open plains of the Central Prairie. From the siege's beginning, trapped garrison members, therefore, early knew what lay in store for them if they surrendered in the upcoming inevitable battle—immediate execution and perhaps even worse, torture.

After all, the Anglo-Celtic soldiers looked upon Mexican soldados as dark-skinned savages, who were little different from Native American warriors in their race-based and xenophobic minds. In consequence, any man who surrendered on the morning March 6 already believed that he knew his own tragic fate. Therefore, to their way of thinking, it made no sense for the Alamo men to surrender at all under the circumstances, because it was folly given Santa Anna's no quarter policy.

General Santa Anna, by words and deeds, had made it well known that no mercy was to be expected "for traitors" to the Republic of Mexico. Anglo-Celtics were not only considered traitors and Protestant heretics, but also seen as nothing more than illegal mercenaries, adventurers, land-hungry opportunists, and interventionists (which was mostly the case as relatively few native Texans were garrison members of the Alamo), because they were not Texas colonists, but recent arrivals from the United States. Santa Anna and his officers simply called the Texas revolutionaries and United States volunteers as "land pirates" and with ample justification.

Young Lieutenant Colonel William Barret Travis, a regular Texas Army officer of the cavalry (the Texas Legion) who had been born in the rolling hills of the South Carolina Piedmont, took command on February 24—the siege's second day—when his older co-commander and volunteer officer, James Bowie, fell ill.

On this memorable day which was the first full day of the siege of the Alamo, Travis penned a desperate appeal for reinforcements in an eloquent letter: "The enemy has demanded a surrender at discretion, otherwise, the garrison are to be put to the sword, if the fort is taken." In his famous February 24, 1836 letter, Travis also referred to the Mexicans as a "Gothic enemy" from times past.

Therefore, as Travis explained and all garrison members realized day after day throughout the entire siege, there simply could be no surrender for any garrison members and everyone at the Alamo fully realized as much from the beginning.

If any garrison members thought otherwise about Santa Anna's future intentions, if not bloodlust, about the desire for revenge then they only had to look to the west and see the large red flag of no quarter flying high and proudly from the bell tower of San Fernándo Church during the siege. Quite simply, there would be no surrender for the highest-ranking officer, Lieutenant Colonel Travis, to the most humble and lowest private in the ranks, including Crockett, of the tiny Alamo garrison, and everyone on both sides realized as much from the beginning.

Clearly, Santa Anna was determined to crush this Anglo-Celtic rebellion in the most brutal way possible to save Texas for Mexico, and the systematic use of terror, especially the no quarter policy, had been decided upon as part of the military strategy to achieve decisive victory north of the Río Grande River.

In this sense, the Alamo garrison was merely a pawn in Santa Anna's overall political and psychological strategy, and the wiping out of all the so-called "land pirates" was seen as most appropriate. Most of all, this harsh measure was meant to provide a brutal example and warning to others about the high price of embarking upon rebellion on Texas soil.

Therefore, in the end, the alleged capture of Crockett was highly unlikely, if not entirely impossible, under these strict circumstances of the brutal no-quarter reality and in the chaotic confusion of battle, especially inside the darkened rooms in rear of the church, where Crockett and his men retired toward from their initial defensive position of the low palisade next to the old Franciscan church of cut limestone.

But some of Captain Harrison's Tennessee men remained at their assigned defensive position at the low palisade and died defending it to the last. However, most of the Tennesseans were killed at both places—before the church and at or near the palisade--during the course of the battle because of its fluidity and fast-pace, after the north wall was breached.

Even more, Crockett was not known to either Santa Anna or his men, including officers, because they were people of another race, religion, country, and culture that existed far outside the mainstream of United States culture. Unlike the strange situation in Hancock's film in which even the illiterate soldados of the lowly peasantry were depicted as having been familiar with Crockett and his lofty legend evidently from having read his popular books, including his popular autobiography *A Narrative of the Life of David Crockett of the State of Tennessee* (1834), United States newspapers, and the *Crockett Almanacs* (first published in 1835), or had even closely followed his political career—first as a Tennessee legislator in the 1820s and then as a Tennessee Congressman in the House of Representatives in 1827.

Of course, such was not the case. Any recognition or knowledge of Crockett among Santa Anna's men, including officers, because any such extensive knowledge of American culture and politics firmly rooted in Mexican culture as depicted would have been an utter impossibility.

In total, four Crockett books were published in his name by eastern ghostwriters, except his popular autobiography because he made significant contributions to the narrative. These works were published between 1833 and 1836 by his Whig promoters for political reasons in opposing President Jackson and for profits by exploiting Crockett's popularity among Americans.

Such books, of course, had never been read by Santa Anna's men, except perhaps by an educated officer like Colonel

Almonte, who spent time in the United States. However, there is no direct evidence, especially from primary sources, that Santa Anna or any of his officers, including Almonte who made no mention of Crockett's capture or execution in his journal for March 6, had read anything about Crockett's reputation and career in the United States.

The longtime assumption has remained that Crockett had been identified by the fighting men of Mexico when he was allegedly captured, and as indicted by some Mexican Crockett execution accounts that were written after the war. But how could have the original information about Crockett's alleged surrender and execution have been circulated by Mexican soldiers—not the relatively few Alamo Anglo-Celtic and black, like Joe, survivors who were entirely silent on this subject of execution—, if they had been unable to identify Crockett in the first place, since they, including Santa Anna, knew nothing about him and had never seen any paintings or sketches of him?

In the end, who had really seen Crockett's alleged execution on the bloody morning of March 6, 1836? First, no American survivors like Joe (Travis' Alabama-born slave) or Susanna Dickinson, who failed to mention any such execution after the battle, ever said anything about executions for their entire lives.

As mentioned, if Crockett had been executed after the battle, then the Alamo's noncombatant survivors, especially Susanna and Joe, would have either seen it or almost immediately learned about it. De la Peña, as revealed in a controversial entry of a single paragraph in his postwar memoir that suddenly appeared in Mexico City in 1955, claimed to have witnessed the event. But was this situation actually the case?

However, de la Peña claimed to have turned from the ugly scene of Crockett's alleged execution at the last second, which meant that he never saw the killing of the prisoners. Was this a way for de la Peña, a military man of honor and high moral character, to justify the writing of the paragraph from another Mexican account or newspaper by truthfully admitting that he never saw the execution of prisoners, including Crockett? Or did de la Peña simply use postwar Mexican and newspaper accounts of Crockett's execution when expanding his journal into book form during the years of rewriting his manuscript after the Texas Revolution?

Significantly, however, no words about Crockett's alleged execution appeared in any Mexican battle report, including that of Santa Anna who wrote his first one on the same day, March 6, not long after the Alamo's fall. Certainly, Santa Anna would have written about Crockett's death in his report to prove outside interference—like the captured blue flag of the New Orleans Grays--and foreign intervention from the United States to show the people of Mexico and his fellow politicians in Mexico City exactly who was really supporting the revolt at this time—not Texas colonists but mostly recent arrivals from the United States like Crockett.

As mentioned, the news of Crockett's death at the Alamo would have been propaganda gold for Santa Anna, because the Tennessean was an international figure, who was well-known on both sides of the Atlantic. But Santa Anna and his officers wrote nothing on March 6 about the execution of the most famous man at the Alamo. As noted, Almonte's journal remained entirely silent on this subject as if it never happened, which was the case.

Indeed, the real answer to his long-existing mystery and source of endless debate about who had actually witnessed Crockett's alleged execution on the bloody morning of March 6, 1836 is a basic and simple one—no one at all, because Crockett's execution simply never happened as long alleged by Mexican sources from the postwar period.

Chapter I

"The Man from the Cane" and his Last Hunting Trip

In truth, David Crockett's death by alleged execution in the immediate aftermath of the Alamo's fall has been an enduring myth, which has grown in recent years to reach new heights because it has now become fashionable.

This old tale—one that has existed since 1836--most recently came alive in full force. It was resurrected with the American publication of the José Enrique de la Peña memoir in 1975, after having been translated from Spanish to English. But in truth, the story of Crockett's alleged execution has been actually nothing more than another Alamo myth in a very long list of myths about this famous battle—like so much about Crockett's life, even when he was alive in the tradition of the *Crockett Almanacs*.

As noted in following on the heels of the greater general acceptance of the de la Peña memoir since 1975, this resurrected rumor that has evolved into a myth reached its peak with the release of the 2004 John Lee Hancock film *The Alamo.*

And like the Crockett execution myth, a good many other myths about Crockett in Texas and his very short period of service—less than a month from February 8, 1836 to March 6, 1836—at the Alamo have survived to this day. As a popular frontier symbol on a national level during his own lifetime, Crockett experienced the bewildering development of having been saddled with two distinct personas that had resulted in considerable confusion in regard to the truth by so thoroughly mixing up of the historical facts with the romantic legend.

But it was this mythical Crockett that proved successful in propelling his political career to new heights. The real, or historical, Crockett, and the mythical, or fictional, Crockett often blended into one to thoroughly muddle the facts and realities to create a mystery man in actuality, because of the wide contradictions between the two personas.

First and foremost, the initial myth about Crockett and Texas, including the story of the Alamo, has distorted the most fundamental reason why the Tennessean from the most humble of origins on the remote western frontier decided to ride southwest from his West Tennessee home and all the way to the Mexican-owned land of Tejas, of Texas.

The very reason why Crockett started off to Texas in the first place on the first day of November 1835 and ended up at the Alamo had little, if anything, at all to do with the Texas Revolution, which had erupted at the small Texas town of Gonzales, just east of San Antonio de Béxar , in early October 1835. At this time because the Texas Revolution had just begun, Crockett had little, if any at all, information about developments, especially revolutionary ones, in far-away Texas, while living on the isolated western frontier in West Tennessee.

When Crockett, who had been just defeated in his summer 1835 bid to regain a seat in Congress, rode away from his home in Weakley County, West Tennessee, with Lindsey K. Tinkle, nephew William Patton, and Abner Burgis, Crockett's brother-in-law who was married to his wife's sister Margaret, on November 1, 1835, he did so with a hunting trip and a burning desire to explore the Red River country of east Texas in mind.

But in truth, he was more on the hunt for fertile acres of east Texas land than game like deer and buffalo, although he was determined to go after both during his fact-finding expedition far from home. These were the primary objectives of Crockett and his friends in riding all the way to the unspoiled Red River country, which was located just beyond the United States border, and nothing more. This was a time of personal pleasure so that Crockett and fellow adventurers could hunt and enjoy themselves in their favorite past time, while exploring a new country that was far more beautiful and pristine than the wilds of West Tennessee.

Indeed, this lengthy trek to Texas was not just another hunting trip as in the past, because it was most of all about prospects for the future. With confidence and hoping for the best after the ruin of his political career in Washington D.C., Crockett rode forth on a trip of exploration to find a new land of plenty and opportunity to eventually bring his family and members of the Patton clan (his in-laws) with him to the Red River country. In soaring spirits, Crockett's own excited words—the old David was back in a rather remarkable personal resurrection with a brighter future--about discovering what was a natural paradise from one of his letters has revealed as much.

Ever the explorer and hunter of new lands untouched by the corrupting influences of so-called civilization, Crocket was astounded by what he saw around him upon crossing the Red

River into east Texas from the north. In glowing terms, he described the Red River country as "the garden spot of the world."

Crockett marveled at the sheer beauty of this undeveloped land owned by Mexico, which had almost inexplicably neglected to settle and exploit this fertile area, that stood just across the border on the west side of the Red River. With clarity mixed with excitement fueled by the seemingly endless tantalizing possibilities, he envisioned settling in this lush region that offered everything that he had long desired in his life, after deciding that his life in the United States, especially in political terms, was over for all practical purposes.

As Crockett emphasized to his West Tennessee family back home in his letter, this picturesque, bountiful wilderness consisted of "good land and plenty of timber and the best springs . . . good range, clear water [unlike the chocolate-colored Obrion River of his West Tennessee homeland] and every appearance of good health and game aplenty [and] It is the pass where the buffalo passes from the north to the south twice a year, and bees and honey plenty."

Crockett was obsessed with gaining a "league of land" in Texas. As he wrote to a family member: "I expect in all probability to settle on the Border of the Chactaw [Choctaw]

Bro [Bayou] of [the] Red River that I have no doubt is the richest country in the world."

Quite simply, this scenic part of east Texas was the world of milk and honey that he had been searching for his entire life. And now Crockett had found it in the picturesque Red River Valley, where he and his comrades enjoyed hunting buffalo, the fabled migratory animal and "King" of the southern Great Plains, for the first time in their lives.

The myth has long existed—from 1836 to even this late day in the twenty-first century—that Crockett rode to the Texas on a great patriotic mission for the express purpose of joining the ranks of the Texas Army and fighting for liberty at the Alamo. But such was simply not the case, and this assumption was only part of the mythical Alamo.

In fact, joining the fight in Texas and especially getting trapped at the Alamo were naturally the last thoughts on Crockett's mind when he had prepared for his next adventure, and one that he hoped would be his greatest. With a nice literary career in the United States with multiple popular books to his name, including best sellers, Crockett believed that his forthcoming adventures in Texas would eventually translate into another best seller and one in which would be extremely popular with the American public. Indeed, Americans were fascinated with Texas, which they hoped would eventually be secured by the United States in the Manifest Destiny tradition and the westward push to the shining waters of the Pacific Ocean.

Despite a prized possession of Mexico and jealously guarded by far-away Mexico City, Texas was a popular topic across America. After all, it was widely believed that Texas had been part of the Thomas Jefferson's Louisiana Purchase from Napoleon Bonaparte in 1803 and, therefore, it was still part of the United States, and not Mexico, which had gained its independence from Spain in 1821.

Crockett, still a poor man who struggled most of his life with finances and despite a prominent national figure, saw a way to make money with a Texas book like his other four previous books, which had been eagerly purchased by an admiring public. Three of these books had been written by others, or ghostwriters, and he had received considerable assistance from another writer, well-educated Thomas Chilton, for his 1834 autobiography *A Narrative of the Life of David Crockett of the State of Tennessee.*

Despite the abundant facts, including his own letters from Texas that were unwarlike, that have indicated otherwise, one of the core Alamo myths was that Crockett made his decision to fight for Texas liberty while still in West Tennessee, and that it was this burning republican faith and love of liberty that eventually led him straight into the deathtrap, the old Franciscan mission known as the Alamo.

But the longtime general assumption that he journeyed to Texas for the express purpose of battling for liberty by joining the Texas Army—which he did in east Texas, in mid-January 1836 after having left home on November 1, 1835—and battling for the cause of Texas independence has no basis in fact or historical evidence.

At some point while exploring the lands in Texas along the border in the Sabine River country and hunting all manner of game, including buffalo, that was in great abundance, Crockett had learned about the October 1835 opening of the Texas Revolution and how the newly-forming Texas revolutionary government was offering thousands of acres for any American who would enlist in the cause of Texas. This exciting news completely altered Crockett's plans and ultimate destiny in the end, sending him and his comrades to the mostly Tejano town of Nacogdoches, which was located just west of the United States-Mexico border, the Sabine River.

Indeed, this long-accepted and generally assumed chief motivation of going to Texas for the express purpose of fighting for liberty as a super patriot was never the case for the middle-aged Crockett, who was a bit too old for active military service at age 49. But he had fought Native Americans, the Creeks, as a younger man in the western frontier tradition that was a rite of passage. The bloody Creek War of 1813-1814 was actually part of America's longest war in battling against the native inhabitants across the breath of America from the Atlantic to the Pacific.

Even more, Crockett had no intention or plans of ever enlisting as a lowly Texas private—a somewhat embarrassing, if not humbling, low rank for a savvy Creek War veteran with a lofty reputation as a so-called colonel, his legendary combat prowess, and a former senator from the halls of Congress—when he left home in Weakley County, Tennessee.

In addition, some evidence exists that Crockett was war-weary and even haunted to a degree by the horrors that he had witnessed, including the killing of Native American women and children, while serving under General Andrew Jackson during the Creek War of 1814. By early 1836, Crockett was carefree and heady over the prospects for the future because the intoxicating idea of a new life, including a possible political career in Texas, had intoxicated him with new life and energy.

Crockett's optimistic and humorous personality came alive when engaged in active campaigning in the open air and when on the march against the enemies of his people, especially the Scotch-Irish settlers of the frontier, acting as a tonic to him. In regard to his early service in the Creek War (1813-1814) which was a sub-conflict within the overall context of the War of 1812, or the Second War for Independence, he was described as "the merriest of the merry, keeping the camp alive with his quaint conceits and marvelous narratives," for which he was destined to become well known in the future on the national stage.

For the young Tennessee frontiersmen, beginning at age 27 in 1813, and like for any hardened veteran of a ruthless war, especially one between different races and cultures in which little mercy was shown by either side like during the Texas Revolution, these searing experiences of the Creek War were traumatic to the point that Crockett very likely suffered from nightmares about the war's horrors.

These surreal horrors of war included the systematic slaughtering of Creeks, including women and children who were killed in some cases either by accident or design, without mercy in the frontier tradition of a brutal total war. As a tall and thin teenager, Andy Jackson, who was of Scotch-Irish descent like Crockett, had endured his own horrors of war during the American Revolution in South Carolina, where all of his family members perished, and he emerged from the war as an impoverished orphan.

Crockett was part of Jackson's force of Tennesseans who won the first victory of the Creek War deep while serving deep in the wilderness of today's Alabama on November 3, 1813. Describing the bloody Battle of Tallusahatchee in which Jackson won his first success of the Creek War, Crockett wrote how: "We now shot them down like dogs; and then set the [log] house [in the village] on fire, and burned it up with forty-six warriors in it."

For a host of reasons and almost certainly, consequently, the very last objective that Crockett desired in November 1835 was to engage in yet another war in a far-away land against an unfamiliar people of a different race and culture at age forty-nine. Now stout from having put on extra weight in his maturity, he was considered an old man by the young folks at this time, when lifespans were generally much shorter than today. At the Alamo, therefore, Crockett was now longer the trim, athletic, and muscular frontiersman that he had been when a young soldier of the Creek War.

Indeed, since he had first departed Winchester, Franklin County, south central Tennessee, after the patriotic call for volunteers in response to the massacre of several hundred whites and mixed bloods (or technically mestizos who were the children of whites and Indians) tat Fort Mims, Alabama, on August 30, 1813 to initiate the Creek War, Crockett had grown less agile and less fit over years of softer living, especially as a Congressman in Washington, D.C.

Quite simply, by 1836, Crockett had long ago lost his prime since he had been a slim and trim fighting man in the enlisted ranks at the Battle of Tallusahatchee, when the hard-hitting General Jackson and the Tennesseans gained bloody revenge on the "Red Stick" Creeks for the massacre at Fort Mims, which had inflamed the people of the frontier, including Crockett and his neighbors.

A fact of which he was only too well aware, Crockett had already risked his life numerous times in the bloody days of the Creek War during two terms of service that stretched from different periods in 1813 to 1815. He knew that he had been extremely lucky in having survived his harrowing ordeal of military service, even during the relatively short duty of his initial period of military service of only ninety days.

But neither a Creek arrow, bullet, or tomahawk had laid him low in the largest battle in which he fought as a private under Jackson in the retributive massacre for Fort Mims at the bloody field of Tallusahatchee. Even more fortunate for Crockett, he had not fallen victim to the greatest killer of them all to soldiers of all ages in the field during the Creek War, the cruel ravages of disease.

However, Crockett had nearly died of disease on his solo return journey back to Tennessee from Jackson's campaign in Florida that had targeted refugee Creeks (the war faction known as the Red Sticks), escaped slaves, and especially Spanish-held Pensacola, after the Creek's decisive defeat at Horseshoe Bend.

In this sense and because of numerous close calls, Crockett was the ultimate survivor of some of the most vicious combat in America that was very much of a racial war. Like many veterans who had survived near brushes with death, therefore, Crockett certainly felt that he was only borrowed time, after having witnessed the disease and battlefield deaths of friends and neighbors during the Creek War.

Having survived quite a few close calls with death in the past and as a proud veteran of the Creek War, Crockett had considerably matured since those bloody days of combat in today's Alabama and in Spanish Florida. By 1836, the former Congressman no longer took life for granted, after having learned all about the surreal horrors of war.

Also negating any consideration that he went to Texas to fight in a new war against the forces of Mexico, Crockett certainly felt no need to demonstrate any kind of youthful bravado and combat prowess like during his teenage years now that he was a mature man and a bit overweight and paunchy at nearly age 50.

As early as 1818, Crockett admitted with candor and honesty that he had no love for military glory or desire for achieving high rank, after having witnessed the nightmarish Creek War during multiple terms of service: "I thought I had done my share of fighting, and that I wanted nothing to do with military appearance."

In these few words, Crockett revealed that his popular image as the consummate warrior and legendary frontier fighter by way of both instinct and inclination was a romantic myth during his post-Creek War years. And, as noted, this situation was particularly the case in his decision to journey to Texas for the express purpose of allegedly fighting the Mexicans in the name of freedom and democracy.

As noted and contrary to the seemingly endless romantic myths and legends that have so often obscured the real man and former Congressman from Tennessee, Crockett was already well past his prime since his Creek War, or glory, days, which were in a previous generation. The lure of land was the great pull for Crockett in 1836, and ultimately determined his fate.

With high expectations, he journeyed to Texas from his home in the Obion River country, which he had first explored in 1821, just after his first session of representing Hickman and Lawrence Counties in the Tennessee State Legislature in mid-November, before moving there. Muddy and slow-moving, the Obion River flowed into the Mississippi from northwest Tennessee. And this unruly West Tennessee river looked quite unlike the spring-fed and clear streams, rivers, and lakes of east Texas.

Indeed, at this time and most of all, Crockett certainly had no reason to press his luck or go against the omnipresent law of percentages by engaging in yet another far-away war—a foreign conflict on Mexican soil and one that he knew little, if anything, about—in a strange land that he had never seen before. Indeed, at this time, he knew relatively little, if anything, about Mexicans and Tejanos, which were all foreign to him, before he departed West Tennessee.

In early November 1835 and as a savvy veteran of the Creek War, the very last thing on Crockett's mind had been in foolishly risking his life in Texas for a cause in which he had no real stake at this time. By this time, he appreciated the fact that life was short.

Contrary to the romantic myths and as noted, Crockett was not motivated by a sense of patriotism or what was later called the intoxicating spirt of Manifest Destiny—the alleged natural and divine right for the United States to simply overwhelm and keep permanent possession of the homelands of other people and nations in the westward push to reach the Pacific shore—or any kind of racism against any people with a darker skin.

In identifying with the carefree lifestyles of Native Americans and their cultural ways and love of nature, Crockett was not a racist, although he had served in a racial conflict— the Creek War. He explained his motivations for going to war in simple terms like other young men of the western frontier: "But my countrymen had been murdered [at Fort Mims}, and I knew that the next thing would be that Indians would been scalping the women and children all about there if we didn't put a stop to it." This ugly reality was just a fact of the brutal fatality of life on the exposed western frontier for generations.

In fact, over time, Crockett became increasingly sympathetic to Native Americans, especially the Creeks who he had helped to defeat as a young Tennessee volunteer during two periods of service. Even the battle-hardened General Jackson, who still carried facial scars when struck by the sword of an angry British officer because of his stubborn defiance in refusing to obey the Briton's humiliating demand to clean his muddy leather boots in South Carolina during the American Revolution, felt sufficient compassion to adopt a Creek infant boy, who had been abandoned by his own people for whatever reason.

Despite the fact that a party of Creeks and Cherokee had killed his Irish grandfather and grandmother in their own log cabin home in a remote section of East Tennessee, Crockett felt sympathy for the Creek people of mostly Alabama, especially after they were decisively vanquished by Jackson's hard-hitting tactics. A man of compassion, he closely identified with warrior ways and Native American values and lifestyles and closeness to the world of nature, including aspects that he deemed superior to white ways.

In systematic fashion, the Creeks were overwhelmed by the forces, both militia and regulars, of General Jackson, whose aggressiveness and ruthless style of frontier warfare could not be matched. Jackson's combative nature was a perfect fit for the overall high caliber—not in appearances but certainly in regard to high-quality battlefield performances--of his tough fighting men, especially volunteers from Tennessee like Crockett. And Jackson continued to prove to be a determined fighter while serving as the president during his fierce political battles that nearly rivaled the nightmarish Battle of Horseshoe Bend, which had been fought in late March 1814, in sheer intensity.

Along with having neglected his Congressional duties for too long in Washington, D.C. in part to promote his popular books and growing national celebrity, Crockett was voted out of office in the summer of 1835 by his fellow West Tennessee citizens partly because he strongly opposed President Jackson's Indian Removal Bill, beginning in 1830 after he split with Jackson in 1829.

President Jackson's harsh Indian Removal Bill led to the disastrous consequences for Native American people, including the confiscation of millions of acres of Indian lands east of the

Mississippi, while sending them west of the Mississippi during the infamous Trail of Tears.

However and as mentioned, Crockett possessed no hatred of either Native Americans or Mexicans, who were mostly a mixed-race people with Indian blood, which served as no incentive for him to possess any culturally- or racially-based enthusiasm to join the fight against another dark-hued people in Texas. For the most part, Crockett felt that Native Americans were much like impoverished whites on the western frontier—all poor people simply struggling against the odds to survive in the wilderness, while living close to the world of nature.

Despite the seemingly endless amount of fiction written about Crockett's life both before and after his death, he was sympathetic toward Native Americans partly because a group of Indians had once saved his life when he had been seriously ill and starving, while on his own far from his Tennessee home.

This timely and invaluable assistance, when journeying back north in attempting to safely return to Tennessee from demanding militia service in Florida under Jackson very likely saved Crockett's life. If not for the compassion of these Indians who he had accidently met on his return journey to his home, Crockett might well have died, and, thereafter, not even have warranted a footnote in history, if he had succumbed on the long trip by himself in the middle of nowhere.

And, of course, Crockett never had any intention of riding all the way to San Antonio de Béxar, Texas—more than 850 miles from his West Tennessee home—with far too few men (only he and nephew William Patton had signed enlistment papers in east Texas in mid-January 1836) and allowing himself to be caught in a deathtrap and surrounded by thousands of Mexican troops, who were ordered to kill every garrison member of the Alamo. Indeed, the popular Tennessean, well known across America for his cutting sense of humor—typically Scotch-Irish--and commonsense stemming from his life on the western frontier experience, possessed no death wish on any kind.

As noted, Crockett only trekked to Texas in large part to enjoy a long life in a new land of "milk and honey," after his seemingly endless struggles as a poor man—the son of a lowly Scotch-Irish immigrant—for nearly his entire life in Tennessee. In this sense, Crockett had still not escaped his lowly-Scotch-Irish roots in the United States, except, of course, in the political field, when he became a Tennessee Congressman.

After his humiliating summer of 1835 defeat to Adam Huntsman during his ill-fated bid to win another seat in Congress, Crockett had completely turned his back on his former life, political career in the United States, and even his beloved West Tennessee, because he was overwhelmed with the intoxicating dream of starting a new life in Texas, and prosperous one unlike merely existing for decades in the United States.

Despite having served as a Tennessee Congressman but without distinction when it came to passing his favorite legislation to justify his lofty political position to serve the people and as expected by his West Tennessee voters, Crockett had his fill of the self-serving and lying politicians of the political elite and propertied class of power and prestige. He especially detested the privileged political antics that he saw Washington, D.C., which was corrupt and self-serving and seemingly to no end. It had been these elitist types of a higher class who had always looked down in contempt at poor westerners, especially the many struggling settlers of Scotch-Irish descent, of the frontier, including Crockett.

As the joke-cracking and homespun frontiersman for which he was well-known in his ongoing political struggles in Congress to defend poor farmers with little land, squatters, and disadvantaged people on the western frontier, Crockett had been sickened by the extent of the greedy ambitions of the elite political class that dominated life in the nation's capital on the Potomac River.

Most of all and to his great credit, Crockett was an honest man who proved to be immune from the usual corruption of the nation's capital. To his dying day, he maintained his lofty principles and personal integrity that revealed the content of character.

Despite his years in politics and in Washington, D.C., he had refused to be corrupted like so many others by what he saw and experienced around him, while representing his beloved West Tennesseans. In this regard, Crockett remained true to himself and his constituents, while his hatred for the intransigence of Congress and the inherent evils of corrupt political life in Washington, D.C., reached new highs during the mid-1830s.

In part because he would not be corrupted and had defiantly remained his own man by standing up for poor settlers, squatters, and farmers of West Tennessee against the powerful political machine of President Andrew Jackson, he had been voted out of office for the second and last time in 1835 to end his once promising career, and even some Whig Party talk about a possible presidential campaign for him to run against Jackson in the future.

But in the end, Crockett's fate was a tragic one, because he never fulfilled his lofty political and personal ambitions, after he was sent packing from office by his own West County constituents because of his ineffectiveness as a Congressman and his intense hatred of Jackson—basically part of his longtime anti-authoritarian streak that partly went back to problems with his own father—which basically backfired on him. Crockett's intense anti-Jackson streak was not shared by his fellow West Tennesseans on the western frontier.

In the end, the combination of Crockett's impassioned independent streak and intense opposition to President Jackson, which became an obsession that made him an angry man to a degree, was too much for his constituents, who he had deviated from in regard to common political beliefs during the Age of Jackson. In boldly confronting America's wartime hero and idol of the common people, Crockett even lost a good deal of his famous good humor (a mixture of western frontier humor and Scotch-Irish humor) that turned into bitterness toward President Jackson and his diabolical political machine that ultimately crushed him and his future prospects.

Even more, the independent-minded Tennessean's wrecked political career—as Jackson had long wished and delighted in his political fall because Crockett had become too popular on the national stage—also sent him in an entirely new direction to the southwest and to the final frontier that now existed for primarily Southerners, who had journeyed across the Red and Sabine Rivers from Louisiana and into the Mexican state of Texas since the early 1820s.

For Crockett and large numbers of lower-class Americans, Texas presented the golden opportunity of gaining more acres than what was even imaginable back in West Tennessee. Clearly, Crockett possessed a love-hated relationship with Washington, D.C., where he had gained national fame and enjoyed a good life when not feuding with Jackson and his powerful supporters.

Like Pennsylvania-born Daniel Boone who had crossed the Mississippi to find his final frontier in Spanish Missouri, so it was time for Crockett to depart what had become an old frontier—the worn and already-settled lands along the brownish Obion River in northwest Tennessee—compared to when he had first seen it in 1821, and head for a new frontier far-away. The seemingly endless opportunities of Texas had long been on Crockett's mind like so many other Americans, especially members of the lower class.

Back in 1834 and one year before the outbreak of the Texas Revolution, he had met with Sam Houston, another former soldier (an ex-lieutenant of a United States regular regiment) under Andy Jackson during the Creek War and six years younger than Crockett who served as a volunteer, in Washington, D.C. At that time, they talked about Texas at great length, and Crockett learned first-hand that this was the Promised Land.

Despite having been known as the "Big Drunk" among the East Tennessee Cherokee who had lived with for three years as a younger man, Houston was Jackson's dependable right-hand man and agent for wrestling Texas away from Mexico in the name of Manifest Destiny, because the South Carolina-born president (Crockett had been born in East Tennessee) had long coveted Texas to become part of the republic.

Most of all, Crockett was determined to escape the haunting political, personal, and family—he was neither a good husband or family man because of his long absences and irresponsible ways which were that of a typical frontiersman—failures of his past and the total collapse of his political career with his 1835 defeat to Adam Huntsman in the bid for another Congressional term of office.

For these reasons, Crockett was adamant in looking forward to life in a new land to fulfill his earlier boast for those individuals who had loudly mocked and turned against him, because of his own political mistakes and open defiance of President Jackson, who was the most popular hero of Tennessee, that: "Go to Hell, and that I Would Go to Texas."

Therefore, what Crockett most of all saw in his idealistic vision of the intoxicating dream of Texas was a bright new beginning for him and his family like when he had carved out a new home for his family in the untamed Obion River country. At the time, he considered enlistment not to have been a high risk undertaking—unlike serving as a lowly private and then with a sergeant's rank in the Tennessee militia in 1814 during the Creek War—in aligning himself with Texas revolutionaries, who were trying to steal Mexico's fairest land because they considered it their God-given right in their convoluted nationalist and common racial thinking of the day.

However, the Texas rebels and United States volunteers of early 1836 were still more like farmers than legitimate soldiers in the militia tradition and joining them might well result in a tragic ending for Crockett far from home. But, of course,

Crockett had no idea just how high those odds were against him at the time, because they became extremely one-sided by 1836.

Even more, Crockett's collapsed political career and aspirations to resume it one day in Texas, if given the political opportunity, were last on his list of priorities, because he had become so thoroughly disillusioned by politics in the United States. He had even become completely disgusted with the people of West Tennessee who had voted him out of office largely because he had bravely opposed Jackson's harsh Indian Removal Bill and autocratic measures that he viewed as anti-democratic as the president became more powerful over time.

Indeed, by the time that he started off for Texas on November 1, 1835, the last thing that Crockett desired was to once more engage in another round of ugly politics—Texas revolutionary politicians were especially hot-headed and quarrelsome--and being around more vain, self-serving politicians, who he viewed as upper class elitists and not self-made men like himself.

In this sense, Crockett had in some ways reverted back to his youth—he was now nearly 50 and a bit overweight from the easy, celebrity life in Washington, D.C. and the long period of a heady existence in the decadent east—in which he had always been searching for better land on a new frontier in the West, which presented greater opportunities to him and his family.

In Crockett's mind, youth and a new frontier were basically the same because they equated to a fresh, new beginning, and going to Texas was all about a spiritual and psychological rebirth in which even a hard-luck and poor frontiersman can remake a failed past into a successful future for himself and family. Therefore, the new frontier of Texas represented a resurrection of body, spirit, and soul to Crockett in early November 1835, when he began his journey toward the southwest.

Indeed, what Crockett most of all was searching for--like when he had first explored the Obion River country in the early 1820s when a much young man--was nothing less than a new lease on life, and a new personal legacy that came with a fresh start. And, as a lifelong frontiersman of the West, he had long understood that the key to his and his family's future welfare and happiness, along with a personal rebirth that he badly needed, lay in what was always most valuable to western frontiersmen as long as he could remember and going back generations to his Ireland-born grandparents and long before that time in Ireland: 1) plenty of land of an unspoiled and pristine nature, 2) an ample amount of game to hunt, 3) rich soil for the growing of crops, and, 4) a mild and relatively warm climate.

Most of all, Crockett hoped that Texas might fulfill all of these key requirements for the good life of a western frontier family of modest means, when he eventually planned to move his entire family, including the Patton in-laws, from the Obion River country to east Texas, if this new land looked sufficiently promising and bountiful as he had heard from other Americans, including Sam Houston.

Perhaps most of all, Crockett was searching for his long-lost youth, which was no more than now that he was age 49, by embarking on one final adventure in far-away Texas. Now a middle-aged man and no longer the slender, wiry hunter that he had been in his younger days, Crockett was now about to begin anew like when he had been still a youth, because he was once again starting over in the hope of making things much better for himself and his family in a new land.

A determined Crockett, who had refused to allow his great dream to die and to his credit, wanted to secure what he had always needed in life (a large amount of acres) as long as he could remember. But he could never obtain a sizeable farm despite his best efforts, since he had lived basically as a poor man for his entire life.

And now the golden dream of Texas represented one final opportunity for Crockett to get ahead in life in a sufficient way and improve his social and financial status and that of his family as a large Southern landowner—always the key to future success for a western frontier family—by acquiring a sizeable numbers of acres that he had never been able to obtain along the western frontier of Tennessee.

Ironically, Crockett's Southern roots—rather than frontier-- have long been basically ignored by generations of historians became of his western frontier image, but he possessed typical Southern dreams of advancing in life. Although the son of Irish immigrants, Jackson also possessed the Southern dream, and this ensured that he eventually owned a large plantation, the Hermitage, and many slaves.

Like Crockett, Jackson was a Southerner. Therefore, to Crockett, Texas was not only a golden, but also a fantastic, opportunity like no other that he had ever been presented or imagined possible in his entire life partly because he possessed his own Southern dream.

Typical Scotch-Irish Anti-Authoritarianism

Still another key factor—the most overlooked one by historians—also motivated Crockett to still succeed: his distinctive Scotch-Irish qualities of a strong never-say-die sense of determination born of adversity and hardship like his own Scotch-Irish and Scottish ancestors in Ulster Province, north Ireland. In many ways, Crockett remained much like an aspiring son of Ulster Province, north Ireland.

Perhaps the best example of Crockett's mindset and typical Scotch-Irish personality, especially his defiant anti-authoritarianism to President Jackson, which set him on the path to become a military hero in Texas first took place in February 1823, after he had settled in the Obion River country of northwest Tennessee.

Temporarily getting away from the hardscrabble farm and second wife Elizabeth Patton, who was a business-savvy mate of a class higher than his own in a most advantageous marriage in 1816, and who helped to later fund his political campaigns, after his first wife, Mary, known as Polly, Finley (of Scotch-Irish heritage like Crockett) died in 1815, Crockett's political career actually began when he went to town, Jackson, Tennessee.

97

At that time, he journeyed the around forty miles to Jackson, which was located about 40 miles east of Memphis and served as a major trade center in West Tennessee, not only with his son, John Wesley, but also with a packhorse burdened with a load of skins to sell to the highest bidder in February 1823.

In Jackson which had been named in honor of Andrew Jackson in today's Madison County, Tennessee, he ran into some old friends—fellow Tennessee volunteers from the old days of a decade before—who had also served under Andy Jackson during the Creek War.

Naturally, these veterans of one of the most brutal conflicts in American history went to the nearest tavern to quench their thirst and talk about the old days and good times, when they had reaped glory—although a grisly and bloody one—in battling the Creeks and thoroughly vanquishing them to remove a serious threat in the southeast, because they were natural allies to the British during the War of 1812.

Ironically, this chance meeting in a rustic tavern in Jackson explained how Crockett began his political career in a most unorthodox and unusual fashion. This meeting explained a central mystery about the course of Crockett's life and career as a soldier, politician, and eventually as a celebrated Alamo defender: how could a simple bear hunter and woodsman from the wilds of Tennessee possibly become a frontier icon and then move smoothly into a high level in the political realm and all the way to Washington, D.C. without an education, after wining heated elections over his better qualified rivals?

Crockett's lengthy political career was ultimately launched not by personal ambition or desire, but by a profound sense of vengeance that was a well-known quality of western frontier life and his own personality, which was most often disguised by his humorous, gregarious, and good-natured side of his Scotch-Irish ancestors.

At this time when at Jackson, Crockett was rather vulnerable in personal and psychological terms for a host of reasons. His usual soaring spirits had been battered down from attempting to create a successful livelihood for himself and family that proved all but impossible despite his best efforts, after having just completed his first term in the Tennessee legislature, which he had won in August 1821 to represent Lawrence and Hickman Counties, Tennessee.

While enjoying a bout of drinking at the tavern, the three Creek War veterans, who were all lower class or middle class members which was reflected as much in their talk and garb, were then joined by a trio of gentleman candidates for the state legislature, and they were of a higher class.

These men were better educated and of a higher class than the hardscrabble Crockett and his roughhewn friends, and they possessed a far more promising future. These established men were anything but frontiersmen, and each one was quite proud of that fact. Therefore, when the three proud men entered the tavern to rally voters on their behalf by the usual method of buying drinks, they shortly sat down at Crockett's table with the same goal in mind. This group of new arrivals included a respected physician, Dr. William E. Butler, who was also Andy Jackson's nephew-in-law and a wealthy aristocrat, a respected major, and another prominent citizen. All three men possessed political aspirations in keeping with their elevated status in life.

During the course of an even more freewheeling bout of drinking at the popular tavern, which grew heavier over an extended period of time, either one or more of these esteemed gentlemen badgered Crockett in jest that he should also run for the state legislature as a mocking joke that was presented in subtle fashion and with careful diplomacy, because, of course, the mere thought of an uneducated frontiersman running for office was ludicrous to these refined gentleman.

From the beginning, Crockett understood the depth of their ridicule behind the subtle mockery of the suggestion of a lower-class frontiersman running for office that was best suited for an educated Southern gentleman of reputation and social status.

Intelligent in his own right and full of frontier commonsense for which he was already known, Crockett understood the true meaning of their words, and it angered him because this situation was really all about the issue of class, status, and wealth. But he became even more incensed when one of the gentleman wags later possessed the audacity to include his name as a candidate, which was published in the Jackson newspaper.

Crockett's bold mockers considered this clever jab at him to have been the ultimate joke that David only learned about around a week later when a visitor showed up to his remote log cabin and told him he as now a candidate to the state legislature to his complete surprise. The timely visitor even possessed the local newspaper to prove his point to the shocked Crockett.

In Crockett's own words that explained the beginning of his political career and what had actually fueled his most ambitious undertaking to date that was destined to reach a national level and heights that he had never imagined possible: "I was determined to make it cost the man who had put [my name] there at least the value of the printing, and of the fun he wanted at my expense."

Clearly, Crockett took this mockery from the more refined and wealthier men of a higher class at his expense to heart. He was sufficiently angered to become stubbornly determined to prove them wrong about everything, especially in regard to the level of his intellect and abilities by obtaining a full measure of revenge on them for their arrogance and conceit that had been unfairly directed at him for no good reason.

Consequently, Crockett decided that he would not only run for the office which his so-called "betters" felt that he was totally unqualified to hold, because of his lack of education and raw backwoods ways for which he was known as "the bear hunter, the man from the cane" of the Obion River country. But in the end, it was Crockett who unexpectedly and boldly forged ahead in his revenge-fueled ambition and determination to win the next election and then "sit in the next general assembly!"

A Common Man Rising

Indeed, Crockett defied the odds and won the election to everyone's shock, including himself to a degree. As an uneducated frontiersmen from the wilds of West Tennessee who now enthusiastically represented poor farmers and hunters on a remote fringe of the western settlements located just east of the Mississippi River, Crockett naturally opposed the wealthy planter elites of fertile lands of Middle Tennessee, where Andy Jackson was viewed as a God-like figure and cotton and slaves made fortunes and led to excesses of wealth, pride, and political power. Out of natural instinct in almost a knee-jerk response, Crockett's target was the upper-class elite and large landowners in a case of nothing less than class and economic political warfare on the national political stage.

Thereafter, Crockett's entire personal and political career was based on symbolizing the degree of natural intelligence and resourcefulness of the self-made common man—or ordinary Americans, mostly small farmers and squatters, of the western frontier--, who believed enough in himself to defy and stand up against his alleged social and intellectual superiors of wealth, privilege, high class, and fancy educations, while proving that frontier commonsense and natural intelligence was equal, if not superior, to that of the elitists. As much as anyone in his day, Crockett demonstrated that a feisty, can-do spirit and sense of determination, which was typically Scotch-Irish and from the frontier, was superior the aristocratic ways and haughty arrogance of the established elite of a higher class.

Consequently he enthusiastically mocked and made fun of his political opponents of a higher class by seemingly endless jokes—Crockett's typically Scotch-Irish humor that served him well in life, like his Scotch-Irish commonsense derived from the frontier, was razor-sharp and especially cutting in the sarcastic tradition—during the course of lively campaigning: the secret of his political success that the common people of Tennessee could personally relate to in the most intimate and personal of ways in part because they shared his anti-elitist views and sense of humor, which was that of the common man.

Like Crockett, so the common people of West Tennessee were doers, intelligent in their own ways although largely uneducated, self-sufficient in the frontier tradition, hard-working and resourceful individualists of the soil, and honest without the corrupting and self-serving ways of the wealthy, aristocratic elite of the upper class.

And in much the same way as his unique experience with the three allegedly social and political superiors at the smoke-filled tavern at Jackson, Tennessee, and for basically some the same fundamental reasons, he was now going to Texas to begin anew partly because so many people, including his former supporters in West Tennessee, even now underestimated him and viewed him as a miserable failure unworthy of office or distinction. But as mentioned, whenever people counted Crockett out, he was sure to rise to the occasion, and Texas presented that golden opportunity for resurrection and redemption on a grand scale.

And so, as when he began his political career long ago, Crockett was determined to prove them all wrong once again, after his 1835 Congressional defeat. For this fundamental reason, he even turned his back on the splendid opportunity of serving as a land agent in the unspoiled countryside Red River Valley, the dividing line between Texas and Louisiana, to garner a fair amount of acres. Instead, he boldly decided to go his own way and joined the Texas Army, and then rode even farther southwest, deep into Tejano country, and all the way to San Antonio de Béxar to join the small Anglo-Celtic garrison at the Alamo.

Once Crockett saw what the pristine lands of east Texas had to offer in abundance, he had made his determination not to return to West Tennessee as originally planned when he had departed home on November 1, 1835. He was now fully committed to Texas to the very end of his eventful life.

Still another factor fueled Crockett's determination to go all the way to the Alamo, despite his wife's opinion that he was too old for another risky adventure so far from home when nearly age 50: his literary career needed to be resurrected with a new book.

Still needing money and craving the national fame that he had been long accustomed to while serving in Congress in Washington, D.C., and in becoming a well-known national figure, Crockett was also searching for the kind of exciting adventure that would serve as the basis of his next book, which he naturally hoped would be another best seller. After all, besides a large amount of land, Crockett needed to restore his financial situation, which was in bad shape as throughout most of his life.

Besides gaining a plentiful amount of fertile Texas land that would fulfill a longtime ambition by catapulting him into the ranks of the large landowners and a higher class in the Southern tradition, Crockett saw opportunities and money in the writing of his next book, which was sure to be popular because of the high interest of Americans in Texas. Indeed, at this time, no subject could be more exciting to Americans across the land than Texas and a new war in the southwest that had been initiated by the Anglo-Celtic settlers, including relatives and friends, with Mexico, in early October 1835.

Besides perhaps embarking upon a new political career of a revolutionary government if Texas won its independence from the Republic of Mexico to resurrect his political fortunes that had totally collapsed in the United States, Crockett envisioned nothing less than a future best seller, which would outdo all of his previous books and past literary successes, including best sellers, especially his popular autobiography.

Throughout the past, Alamo historians have most often overlooked this most forgotten reason for Crockett's final fatal decision to fight for Texas and go to the Alamo—to eventually sell books about his upcoming Texas adventure, which would prove fascinating to the American reading public. Ironically, a new book, *Col. Crockett's Exploits and Adventures in Texas, Written by Himself,* was destined to appear in 1836, but it was a hoax, because Crockett died without leaving any account, including letters, about his final days at the Alamo and his last adventure on a distant frontier far from home.

Chapter II

A Rendezvous with Destiny at the Alamo

At the east Texas town of Nacogdoches on January 14, 1836 after his small party had arrived in early January, Crockett's fate was sealed when he and William Patton, his favorite nephew, signed the oath of allegiance to the "Provisional Government of Texas." He now had less than two months to live in a Texas that he had already grown to love.

It was a new start in a military adventure that was most lucrative, if he survived the Texas Revolution, and quite unlike when he had first signed up at age 27 to serve in the Creek War in 1813. Crockett was entitled to a large number of acres (4,600) in Texas, if he faithfully served his term of service of only six months in the cause of Texas.

Like twice during the Creek War, Crockett, at age 49, once again became a soldier as in the more carefree days of his youth, after signing his enlistment papers and swearing a solemn Texas oath of allegiance at Nacogdoches, before the town judge, Ireland-born John Forbes. Judge Forbes had been born to Scottish parents in the town of Cork, southern Ireland. If he learned about the Tennessean's Scotch-Irish roots, Forbes almost certainly appreciated the fact that the Crockett family's roots could be traced back to the Emerald Isle.

In the process of making a life-long dream come true on Texas soil, Crockett now possessed the potential of becoming a large landowner and a rich one if he survived the Texas Revolution to develop his hundreds of acres and raising crops, especially the most lucrative cash crop in Texas, cotton.

Crockett anticipated that his service in Texas would be relatively brief, (he signed up for a term of only six months as a volunteer) easy, and an uneventful one--perhaps no fighting at all--as when he had served (twice from 1813 to 1815) in the ranks of the local Tennessee militia for short periods during the Creek War.

But, unknown to Crockett, the war in Texas was anything but another Creek War in the depths of Alabama, when the hard-fighting Jackson first achieved a national reputation by eliminating the major threat posed by the Creeks during the War of 1812.

After all, by early 1836 when Crockett crossed the Red River and entered an unspoiled Texas, no more Mexican troops remained on Texas soil. Therefore, to Crockett's way of thinking and other volunteers in Texas, there would be no fighting, if the Mexicans decided not to attempt to regain Texas by force—a dangerous assumption and gamble of the first magnitude. But Anglo-Celtic pride and hubris were at such a high that many people believed that Santa Anna would not dare risk invading Texas, because of the alleged ferocity, superiority, and combat prowess of the Anglo-Celts.

It was a heady time in Texas and the level of confidence among the ragtag revolutionaries could not have been higher. General Perfecto Cos and his forces had surrendered to the armed Texas colonists and United States Volunteers during the first fall of the Alamo in December 1835, after the attackers had suffered relatively few losses in capturing San Antonio de Béxar and the Alamo. Then, the defeated Mexicans had been allowed to march south of the Rio Grande River in accordance with the liberal surrender terms, paroles and the traditional honors of war.

The winter of 1836 in east Texas was certainly a glorious time for Crockett that had nothing at all to do with the Texas Revolution, especially after his past disappointments in the United States. But most of all, he and nephew William Patton must have been intoxicated by the mere thought of the nearly

10,000 acres of prime Texas land in total that they would receive for their short-term military service, if they completed their terms of duty.

Clearly, the immense size of Texas meant that land was far easier to obtain and much cheaper than anything that Crockett had ever seen before or had previously imagined possible— about one-tenth the price of public lands for sale in the United States.

In his last letter, which was written on January 9, 1836 at San Augustine, Texas, and with barely two months to live, Crockett penned to his oldest daughter Margaret: "What I have seen of Texas, it is the garden spot of the world, the best land & prospects to any man to come here, and I do believe it is a fortune to any man to come here; there is a world of county to settle, it is not required to pay down for your league of land; every man is entitled to his headright of 4438 A[cres] and they may make the money to pay for it off the land."

But, of course, there was one catch and it was a big one that might one result in one losing one's life in the ongoing Texas Revolution, since Santa Anna would surely launch a counterstroke with large numbers of troops in 1836 because of his burning desire for revenge, although the optimists—hubris now reigned supreme in Texas--believed that this would not be the case.

These precious acres of a beautiful land were still owned by the Republic of Mexico, and Santa Anna and the people of Mexico were determined to get them back at any cost. The Mexican nation and its people were united in refusing to allow the ever-aggressive Anglo-Celtic rebels to steal one of the fairest portions of Mexico from the republic.

If Santa Anna successfully crushed the Texas revolt to keep his republic from losing its most prized possession, then Crockett might be killed or captured during his six-month term of service, and, in the end, never receive a single acre of precious Texas land. First and foremost, the band of Texas revolutionaries and United States volunteers, who had boldly stood up against the might of the central government in Mexico City, had to win their war—no small task under the circumstances that were most unfavorable, if not all but impossible, for the motley, ill-prepared defenders of Texas, especially at the Alamo, if Santa Anna decided to invade with overwhelming numbers.

Not seduced by the bonanza of Texas acres and perhaps worried about what might happen to them so far from home and in the midst of a revolution, Crockett's two other companions, Abner Burgin, Crockett's brother-in-law who was married to his wife's sister, and Lindsey K. Tinkle, a close friend, departed Nacogdoches and headed back home to West Tennessee. They had not been seduced by the lure of Texas acres, if they had signed up and joined the Texas Army.

In doing so, these two wise men unwittingly saved their lives by avoiding the sad fate of getting caught in the swirling vortex and entirely unpredictable currents of the Texas Revolution. But according to his custom and personal motto for which he was famous across the United States, Crockett was determined "to go ahead," because he was sure that he was right, when it came to what he had seen and knew about Texas.

Quite simply, the opportunity provided by Texas was simply too great to pass up for Crockett. In the end, Crockett's own personal Rubicon had come when he crossed the swirling waters of the Red River to gain the south bank and entered Texas. As a cruel fate would have it, Crockett would never leave this land that he loved upon first sight like a teenaged lover of his first girl that he had made love to in the cool of a pine thicket.

After riding southwest from Nacogdoches across the mostly pine woodlands of east Texas and then the grasslands of the sprawling Central Prairie of Texas that seemed to stretch forever and into a deathtrap located just outside of San Antonio de Béxar immediately after the end of the first week in February, Crockett reached the farthest point west that he had ever journeyed from the home that he would never see again.

Clearly, he had overcome countless obstacles in his life and had come a long way from his obscure birthplace in the old Nolichucky settlement, which had been established amid the forested ridges and deep valleys of the Appalachian Mountains during the 1770s in East Tennessee in 1786.

But in the bright sunshine and blue skies of Texas, Crockett seemed to finally be at the end of the rainbow. In his final letter that was written on January 9, 1936 from San Augustine: "I am in great hopes of making a fortune for myself and family" in Texas, and "by way of large land-holdings" of choice Texas acres.

Festive Arrival at a Death-Trap

After another lengthy ride, Crockett arrived at the Alamo on Monday February 8, 1836. As could be expected, he was greeted enthusiastically by the garrison of San Antonio de Béxar. But his luck had already deserted him, although he was not aware of this harsh fact that mocked his seemingly good fortune.

A wild fandango was held in San Antonio de Béxar on the night of February 8 to celebrate Crockett' arrival that lifted the garrison's spirits and gave another good excuse of more dancing, love-making with local Tejano girls, and excessive partying that extended late into the night.

But, in truth, this was not a time for celebration or merrymaking of any kind for these rustic revolutionaries, because a mighty storm was about to descend upon San Antonio de Béxar and the Alamo with a vengeance. Since he had joined the Texas Army in mid-January 1836 and was guaranteed that he would gain large numbers of acres if he fulfilled his terms of service for only six months, Crockett no doubt still felt that he had already won a bonanza of unimaginable proportions. And if he believed that great victories lay in the future like General Jackson's sparkling successes at Tallusahatchee and Horseshoe Bend during the Creek War, then he was sadly mistaken.

However, neither Crockett nor anyone else, including his nephew William Patton, could imagine the awful truth of what was already an excessively dire situation in Texas. The old Spanish mission and its entire garrison of the Alamo were destined to be slaughtered in only twenty-seven days, after the Tennessean's arrival at the Alamo.

Crockett now had less than a month to live on this sweet and fertile soil of Texas, which seemed like an earthy paradise to him. As a cruel fate would have it, Crockett's great dream of embarking upon a promising new start in Texas was fated to end hardly before it had begun and in the cruelest way possible.

By this time, the fragile, ever-feuding revolutionary government of Texas had collapsed and the defenders of Texas, mostly recently arrived men from the United States, were scattered in remote and isolated military outposts, especially at San Antonio de Béxar and Goliad, Texas, southeast of San Antonio de Béxar and near the Gulf of Mexico: easy picking for swiftly-moving Mexican forces, if Santa Anna marched north with a large army to pick off the vulnerable Texas outposts on the frontier one by one.

Like the chaotic Texas revolutionary government situation in which the governor was impeached by angry rival politicians, whose greatest skills lay in personal feuding with each other and displaying immature antics like in a rowdy classroom of juveniles, so the military forces and the inexperienced men who led them were in complete disarray across Texas in a true march of folly.

As could be expected in a new revolution and America's heavy reliance of the militia concept since the days of the

American Revolution, the disorganized defenders of Texas relied upon the people's militia to save the day, which had led to countless internal problems, including mutiny, during the Creek War under Jackson. Therefore, General Jackson had wisely most often relied upon the discipline and dependability of regulars to reap victory in crisis situations: an invaluable lesson that he learned and faithfully continued to utilize when confronting a mighty British invasion force, leading to the winning of the Battle of New Orleans in early January 1815.

For many reasons, the ill-timed reliance upon the old-fashioned militia tradition of the American Revolution and the War of 1812 was ill-suited for the confused situation among the untrained revolutionaries in Texas, especially because Santa Anna now relied heavily on regular troops, because he knew that they could be counted upon. What was needed for the survival of the Texas war effort was an army of regular troops instead of an over-abundance of independent-minded, unruly volunteers.

But the Texans had not the time for such thorough preparations in the organization and training of regular troops during the first winter of the Texas Revolution. When Crockett arrived at the Alamo on February 8 amid a chorus of wild cheering from enthusiastic garrison members, independence had not even been declared by the bickering Texas revolutionaries at Washington-on-the-Brazos.

Ironically, as a balking Tennessee Congressman, Crockett had opposed the first military academy of the United States at West Point, New York, on the premise that the prestigious institution was nothing more than a privileged reserve for the sons of wealthy aristocrats of the upper class, and where they received free educations instead of poor, disadvantaged Americans, who truly needed government assistance in regard to education.

Because of his typical stance of supporting the poor, Crockett strongly advocated for the abolishment of West Point, which created the highly-efficient and well-trained officers of the regular army that were needed to protect the nation— exactly the kind of men who were now necessary to adequately defend Texas in a professional manner unlike the inefficient militia tradition of a bygone age. In this regard, Crockett was entirely wrong in this egalitarian thinking, because West Point ensured not only the winning of the Mexican-American War, but also latter conflicts.

In the upcoming showdown at the Alamo, Santa Anna possessed the advantage of commanding mostly regular troops, who were well-trained, reliable, and experienced: exactly what the undisciplined and untrained Anglo-Celtic volunteers, including those relatively few men who had the misfortune of having been stationed at the Alamo, now needed to adequately defend Texas against a Mexican Army that Santa Anna had smartly based on a highly-efficient Napoleonic model.

In fact, Santa Anna saw himself as the "Napoleon of the West." He had long idolized the native Corsican, whose unlimited personal ambitions of world conquest had led to his ultimate downfall in 1815 like Santa Anna at San Jacinto in April 1836. In much the same way, so Santa Anna's hubris and soaring ambitions led to his decisive defeat at San Jacinto.

The head of the extremely-small Texas regular army at this time, General Sam Houston, President Jackson's man and a longtime active agent for rebellion to fulfill idealistic expansionist dreams of generations of Americans that reached all the way to the White House, attempted to sort out the confusion among the undisciplined volunteers, but to no avail.

Houston, a hero of General Jackson's decisive victory over the "Red Stick" Creeks at Horseshoe Bend, Alabama, when he had served as a young lieutenant of the regular army, had been against the concept of making a defensive stand at the Alamo with too few troops on the exposed, isolated western frontier, knowing that it was absolute folly of the first magnitude.

Unfortunately, for Crockett, he never had an opportunity to consult with Houston, who had been absent from Nacogdoches, to warn him about the disastrous military situation in Texas, including at the Alamo, immediately before the beginning of the 1836 Texas Campaign, when the naïve Tennessean entered Tejas, or Texas, and signed his enlistment papers in mid-January with such high hopes for the future.

Crockett, therefore, remained entirely ignorant of the true military situation and the extent of the dangers, which were already considerable and ever-growing: General Santa Anna was busily preparing to invade Texas with a large army and, as expected, he was set on achieving his own personal revenge for his 1835 losses and thoroughly exploiting the absolutely deplorable civilian and military leadership situation in Texas.

Contrary to myth, Crockett did not bring or command a company of Tennessee Volunteers at the Alamo, as commonly believed. He merely served a "high private" in Captain William B. Harrison's company of 16 men of the Tennessee Mounted Volunteers.

Indeed, David Crockett joined and served in this Tennessee company at the Alamo as nothing more than a "high private," in his own words. This development was in keeping with his national image as a longtime supporter of the common man, who detested the artificiality of higher military rank that allegedly represented a superior individual, because it was anti-democratic and anything but egalitarian in concept. He served with pride as a "high private," despite having been a sergeant twice—two separate terms of enlistment—in the militia during the Creek War more than two decades before.

Captain Harrison's Tennessee boys, including Crockett, were stationed in a vulnerable position, which was to defend the low wall of wooden stakes of the timbered palisade that ran from the southwest corner of the Alamo church to the abode buildings of the low barracks that served as the southern wall. Here, the main entrance of the compound was located in the south wall's center and this entryway was protected by an earthen lunette, which extended beyond the south wall, or low barracks. This key defensive position was the official front door of the Alamo compound, and Harrison's boys, including Crockett, were determined to defend it with their lives.

Complete Surprise of Santa Anna's Sudden Arrival

Crockett had barely arrived less than a month before and he had just settled into life as a private of the Texas Army and garrison duty at the Alamo and San Antonio de Béxar , when Santa Anna caught the entire garrison by surprise on Tuesday

February 23, 1836. Crockett's fate was sealed from that ill-fated day.

After still another wild fandango to celebrate George Washington's birthday on the previous day that continued well into the early morning hours, most of the Anglo-Celtic garrison were sleeping off hangovers and resting that cool Tuesday morning. Some men had spent the night with some of the local black-eyed and long-haired Tejano girls of San Antonio de Béxar, where most of the garrison had their living quarters in the adobe houses of the local residents.

Fortunately for the Alamo garrison, however, a sharp-eyed sentry high in the bell tower of San Fernando Church located on the town's main plaza, which had been erected in typical Spanish style, caught sight around noon of the finely-uniformed men of the Mexican cavalry on the open prairie.

A former dashing cavalryman in his younger days and tactically astute as a general, especially in regard to the cavalry arm, Santa Anna sent an advanced element of his veteran cavalry to surprise the garrison. However, in the nick of time, the suddenly alerted garrison members, evidently including Crockett who stayed with the men of Captain Harrison's company, raced east to the Alamo, before it was too late.

But despite knowing for some time that Santa Anna was headed for San Antonio de Béxar from deep inside Mexico with a new army after Cos' defeat at the Tejano town last December, but believing that he would not strike until April 1836 with the rise of the spring grass on the prairie, relatively little defensive preparations had been made by garrison members for meeting the formidable Army of Operations.

A strange hubris, partly fueled by too much tequila, attractive Latinas, and late night fandangos in the town, had dominated the thinking of overly-confident, naïve Texas leaders and most Alamo garrison members, thanks to the mistaken racial stereotype that one Anglo-Celtic fighting man was equal in quality to ten Mexican soldados.

Of course, such was simply not the case, because this common racial and cultural stereotype of the day was just another popular myth of the Texas Revolution that existed in early 1836. With his ample experience in the Creek War, Crockett most likely knew that this common stereotype was a gross exaggeration, because he had fully appreciated of the excellent performances of Jackson's regular troops during the Creek War. Quite simply, regulars an any army were almost always tough and good fighting men, and Crockett fully realized as much.

This outlandish hubris that infected the Alamo's leaders and garrison members in the face of immense danger and the inevitable arrival of Santa Anna's Army to avenge the defeat of Cos' forces last winter had been once again demonstrated just after Crockett's arrival on February 8. As mentioned, that cold Monday night another wild fandango was held in San Antonio de Béxar for the legendary frontiersman, who was known far and wide for his combat prowess, which only continued to fuel the already heightened overconfidence of a tiny garrison—less than 200 men—that had continued to flirt with disaster on a complete descent into folly.

But now there were no more fandangos or good times for garrison members after the sudden arrival of even more of Santa Anna's troops to surround the Alamo in late February and early March to prevent escape from the mission-turned-fortress, which was much too large to defend with so few men.

Upon first sight of the Alamo compound, Crockett had almost certainly realized as much, because he knew how the Creeks had committed the ultimate tactical folly of having allowed themselves to be surrounded in a fortified position amid a narrow river bend in the shape of a horseshoe (Battle of Horseshoe Bend). In consequence, they had been trapped and slaughtered by the hundreds, when General Jackson had unleashed his regulars, volunteers, and Indian allies.

Even more this completely inadequate defense of a stationary defensive position on the open prairie just outside San Antonio de Béxar was not Crockett's kind of fighting, which was basically irregular warfare out in the open from his days when he served as a private and sergeant in the Creek War. But Crockett was now an official Texas soldier—a mere private in the ranks—since mid-January 1836, and he would do his patriotic duty to the end like during the Creek War in which he had almost lost his life more than once.

Santa Anna's tactical astuteness was revealed by his clever plan of attacking the Alamo that was as detailed as it was precise. He knew that assaulting the Alamo in the daylight hours was folly, and it would result in high losses and almost certain failure in the end. Therefore, only one solution remained for the fulfillment of Santa Anna's masterstroke in offensive tactical terms: a massive assault on all four sides of the Alamo in the darkness just before dawn to catch the defenders in their beds. Consequently, the red sunrise of March 6, 1836 would herald the slaughter of the entire Alamo garrison when caught by surprise, which would be enacted swiftly and brutally.

As he had envisioned with clarity, Santa Anna's insightful tactical plan worked to perfection in the cold darkness before the dawn on March 6. Santa Anna's stealthy scouts killed the handful of pickets stationed in slit trenches that were situated outside of the Alamo's walls in the blackness before the onrush of more than 1,500 troops, who were picked fighting men. Therefore, the sleeping garrison members, who were exhausted from constant labor in strengthening the defenses during the 13-day siege, received no warning from the Alamo's pickets, whose lives and crucial missions were cut short.

Consequently, Santa Anna's surprise was complete in every way, shape, and form, before the cold sunrise of what became a morning in hell. The largest number of attacking Mexican troops concentrated at the north wall, after two other columns had veered toward the north to join the north column of soldados attacking the north wall. Here, an overpowering number of Mexicans were massed and simply could not be repelled, after the garrison had been caught by surprise.

Meeting relatively little resistance, Santa Anna's cheering men then poured over the north wall, brushing aside only a relative handful of defenders, including Lieutenant Colonel William Barret Travis whose bravery in attempting to rally an adequate defense cost him his life at the 3-gun battery located in the center of the north wall. Only a relatively few defenders, like Travis, had been awakened in time at the sounding of the belated first alarm and rushed across the wide plaza to take defensive positions on the north wall.

Withdrawing from the scene of the collapse of resistance, including Lieutenant Colonel Travis' death, at the north wall, surviving defenders fled into the darkened plaza and then took cover in the Long Barracks. Here, they made an effective last stand for some time in their designated secondary defensive position—the Long Barracks--that proved more than adequate rather than attempting to defend the north wall, which was already breached.

Eventually, the Long Barracks, the highest structure of the Alamo compound at two stories, was overwhelmed by the throng of determined soldados, after bloody hand-to-hand combat that very likely took more attackers' lives than even the scaling defense at the walls. On this bloody early morning, the Alamo church of the Franciscan missionaries was the last position to fall in the sprawling compound of around three acres.

It was in this especially vulnerable sector—from the low palisade to the church—that the men of Captain William Harrison's Mounted Tennessee Volunteers, including Crockett, defended from the beginning, and where most of these courageous volunteers died for the golden dream of Texas and a better life in the future. Overwhelmed by a surging tide of soldados, Crockett fell in the open area immediately before the church with most of his men, fighting to the last.

Shocking News Sweeps America

Because he was a national celebrity and famed frontiersman, Crockett's death at the Alamo shocked the nation when newspapers across the United States carried the tragic news. After all, he was a legendary national figure, much like George Armstrong Custer when he was killed at the Little Bighorn by Cheyenne and Sioux warriors—enemies, like Mexicans, that Americans deemed unworthy because of their skin colors and different cultures that were seen as inferior and barbarian--on June 25, 1876, which likewise stunned the America for racial and cultural reasons.

The American republic went into mourning when they heard of Crockett's death, and many "tears [were] shed" across the United States with the disturbing news, which seemed so unfathomable that many Americans refused to believe the truth. Most Americans viewed Crockett's untimely death as a heroic martyrdom in the glorious name of battling for the rights and freedoms of America in a far-away land governed by a corrupt despot, which was partly verified when Santa Anna had first ordered no quarter for the Alamo garrison, including Crockett.

Ironically in the end, Crockett never claimed the thousands of prime Texas acres that were forthcoming for his military service, when that had been his primary motivation to explain why he enlisted and then died at the Alamo, especially in the beginning.

After all, Crockett's lifelong dream was to acquire as many acres as possible to move up the social ladder, and Texas had finally provided him with the realization of that long-sought possibility. But it was an intoxicating dream that never came true for Crockett and other Alamo defenders, when their blood-soaked bodies were piled high upon blazing funeral pyres by the victorious Mexicans and then reduced to ashes on the open prairie outside of the Alamo's walls.

Epilogue

A Dream Deferred

As demonstrated at the Alamo, Crockett's idealistic version of the American Dream, which he had been searching for and trying hard to obtain for his entire life, on Texas soil had an ugly flipside. Indeed, gaining a choice piece of this vast, beautiful land of plenty meant risking one's life on Mexican territory, when the Republic of Mexico was determined to regain its territory from the Anglo-Celtic rebels.

Ironically, although he never realized the fact, including during his long journey to Texas, the frontiersman's great dream had already passed him by in his troubled, hard-luck life, perhaps from the moment that he had been born in the backwoods on August 17, 1786.

By way of a cruel fate, Crockett failed to achieve his American Dream, even as a Congressman who too often forgot his duties to his West Tennessee constituents and neglected his Congressional responsibilities. Crockett's downfall also came because he possessed lowly Scotch-Irish roots and had been a lifelong member of the lower class and then the middle class on the western frontier. Ironically, in the end, he was doomed to die very near the lowly class in which he had been raised in the timbered hills of eastern Tennessee long ago.

Despite all his determined efforts, Crockett had never been able to reach the coveted higher class and status of a proper gentleman planter in the Southern tradition. After his fame as a western frontiersman, Crockett was also a Southerner who possessed distinct Southern values and proclivities.

This lofty vision of aspiring higher in life was first the average Scotch-Irish immigrants' dream of his grandparents and then of the ever-optimistic Tennessean of gaining a higher class from the one in which he had been born: the antitheses of the situation that existed in the stratified, deeply entrenched class structures of Europe, including Ireland that had become England's first colony, that allowed little social mobility.

Nevertheless, to his great credit and to the very end of his life, Crockett never gave up on his tireless efforts of attempting to finally obtain his bright vision of a prosperous American Dream, and he rode to his untimely death at the Alamo in search of the golden dream that promised better days ahead for him and his family as large landowners in Texas and the coveted status of the planter class.

When he rode away from West Tennessee on November 1, 1835 in complete disgust and alienation about political life in the United States, especially in Washington, D.C., he had finally realized that he would never obtain his version of the American Dream not only not in Tennessee, but also not in the United States.

Therefore, for the first time in his life, Crockett had decided that a far-away foreign land now provided the only and last opportunity for him to finally gain large numbers of acres so that he could finally move up the social ladder to planter, or upper class status, to fulfill his goal of reaching out and grabbing the American Dream, but this time on Mexican soil.

Crockett's dogged persistence and never-say-die quest of obtaining the American Dream is not only the real story of his life, but also the real and most forgotten story of his death on March 6, 1836. Indeed, as a poor man, Crockett was forced to take unnecessary and high risks, which, in his case, resulted in an ugly, but heroic, ending for him at the Alamo. Consequently, exactly how Crockett died and if he was executed by Santa Anna as a prisoner or not is not really an important important in the larger context, although the heated debate about the exact nature of his death has long indicated otherwise.

What was most important and the main lesson—that still applies to this day in the twenty-first century for large numbers of immigrants from around the world who migrate to America—of Crockett's life was the fact that he never gave up on the very essence and core meaning of America that was all about searching for greater opportunities and a better life: a belief and faith that had first brought his ancestors all the way from Ulster Province, north Ireland, to rustic settlements on the western frontier, which were extremely vulnerable to sudden Indian attacks that erupted suddenly from the dark forests: the tragic fate of his murdered grandparents, who had been born in Ulster Province, Ireland.

As mentioned, this American Dream was all about the opportunity to improve one's station in life and to finally get ahead by moving up the social ladder, while gaining a level of success unknown to previous generations of the family.

In the end, it was most symbolic that Crockett had ridden farther west—and, of course, then southwest--from his home in West Tennessee and in the same direction as his Scotch-Irish grandparents, who had journeyed west across the Atlantic with high hopes to first settle in 1771 around Lincolnton, North

Carolina, before they met a cruel fate in East Tennessee from Native American raiders. Likewise, this same burning desire for new and better lands led Crockett to push west into today's West Tennessee when still a young man with high hopes and bright envisions of the future.

For both Crockett and his grandparents (Ireland-born David and Elizabeth Crockett) who had been killed in a Creek and Cherokee war party in East Tennessee during the American Revolution in 1777, the greatest of dreams lay in the west and the frontier, and this solitary intoxicating vision never left Crockett's heart or mind as long as he lived.

In this regard, Crockett and his ancestors never lost their same idealistic vision of hope and promise that was provided by a seemingly boundless America, because it was rooted in the same fundamental beliefs that proved timeless, because they were fundamentally rooted in the core concept of the America Dream and the pursuit of happiness, as emphasized by Thomas Jefferson in the Declaration of Independence.

Not only his Scotch-Irish grandparents who lost their lives in the isolated hills of East Tennessee but also Crockett basically sacrificed his life in the end for the same basic reasons, despite the fact that their lives were separated by more than half a century: an idealistic and heartfelt quest to fulfill the same lofty vision and great dream of a brighter future on American soil.

To his credit, Crockett never hated Indians for what they were as a distinctive people with an unique culture or for what they did to his grandparents in East Tennessee during the American Revolution. Especially after the bloodletting of the Creek War, Crockett remained relatively open-minded when it came to Native Americans, despite the trouble that they had caused in his personal life, including even the stern challenge of wartime.

It is now known, but perhaps a haunting guilt over what he and General Jackson's men had done to the Native people during Creek War—very close to what is known today as ethnic cleansing to eventually gain millions of prime acres for white settlement—was increasingly hard to bear for him, as he grew older and wiser about the evils of the world.

But in time, Crockett identified with the tragic plight of Native Americans in bravely fighting a losing battle against the odds and in the face of genocide and the relentless push of too many whites to count. After all, Native Americans were a poor people of the land much like his own Scotch-Irish ancestors from Ulster Province, north Ireland, and Crockett was always in favor of the poor and the underdog—just like himself.

Therefore, in his regard, color was not at all a decisive factor or consideration in Crockett's mind, and not unlike the lack of racial prejudice in regard to the Creeks and other Native Americans, who had long adopted captive whites since the colonial period as full members of their tribe to replace lost loved ones killed in battle in the defense of their people.

Because a hopeful Crockett had ridden southwest for nearly 850 miles to his untimely death on the Central Plains of Texas at an old Spanish mission in his relentless search of fulfilling his American Dream, his final demise at the Alamo was not only tragic, but also quite sad in many ways. After all, a cruel fate, hard luck, a life of frustration largely due to lowly Scotch-Irish roots, a hardscrabble frontier life, and the fickle, corrupted politics of Washington, D.C., created a perfect storm for him that was almost as responsible for his ultimate death, as the final assault of Santa Anna's forces on the early morning of March 6, 1836.

In the end and as noted, what was most important for the historical record was not how Crockett died—Alamo historians have long missed this fundamental point in this regard during the long-existing and quite heated debate about exactly how he met his tragic fate, especially if he was executed on Santa Anna's orders or not—, but for what reasons that best explained why he ultimately died, which had relatively little to do with the concept of patriotism in regard to either the United States or Texas in overall and relative terms.

As a strange fate would have it, like many of the soldados in Santa Anna's Army who were former peasants and the mostly farm boys of the Alamo garrison, Crockett was a poor man who was only still struggling to get ahead in life, And, as mentioned, it was the golden promise of Texas that had provided the best opportunity for him to accomplish that great goal during a hardscrabble life in a socially-stratified homeland, where mostly the elite of the planter class prospered unlike the common people of lower classes, who struggled to make a living on the land by persistence and hard work.

In this regard, the fundamental arguments, endless controversy, and even the de la Peña memoir itself are actually nothing more than moot points of either very little or no real meaning. Indeed, the most timeless and important truth about Crockett's death far from home and family was basically the demise of his own personal American Dream—the frontiersman's endless pursuit of discovering a new land of promise and a better day in the future to improve the lives of himself and family members.

Of course, the dream of Texas was resurrected and made permanent by Sam Houston's miracle victory at San Jacinto on April 21, 1836, when Texas was finally permanently won from Mexico. But by then, it was much too late for Crockett and the men of the Alamo.

For such reasons and like so many other Americans of his generation, including President Jackson, Crockett had viewed Texas as a Garden of Eden, or "the garden spot of the world," in his own words, where he could recreate him into a new man by embarking upon an unprecedented success story for himself and his family on Texas soil: the historic calling and beckoning of the western frontier to generations of lower class Americans that he could not ignore, despite his wife Elizabeth's heartfelt appeals—they were all ignored like his decision to serve his country during the Creek War in October and November 1, 1835—for him to stay home in West Tennessee and be content with what they owned.

But this was not enough for him, and Crockett wanted more, much more, after having endured a hardscrabble life on the western frontier, where he had been born on the banks of the Nolichucky River in the hills of eastern Tennessee. So, in the end, he remained true to his dreams and following them all the way to the Alamo, where he died while in pursuit of idealistic visions that burned brightly in his heart and mind.

Indeed, in this sense, Crockett died not only because of the western frontiersman's traditional pursuit of getting ahead and doing better in life like his poor Scotch-Irish ancestors who had long struggled to achieve the same lofty goal, but also the dream of the typical Scotch-Irish immigrants, who had migrated to the frontier before the American Revolution.

As noted, Crockett's grandparents had migrated to America from the green hills of Ulster Province, north Ireland, before the American Revolution. In a strange way, the dream of Ireland-born David and Elizabeth in having migrated to the South—from North Carolina and then Tennessee—was very the same as Crockett's fateful decision to migrate to Texas 1836. And in the end, they all paid with their lives, from grandparents to grandson, for their ambitions and passionate desires to embrace the American Dream to its fullest and at any risk.

Indeed, Crockett died a poor soldier of a lower rank—lower than when he had served during the Creek War as a private and then a sergeant—not unlike his grandparents who had been forced to migrate from north Ireland because they had been poor and part of the lower class without property or future prospects.

In the end, Crockett remained a common man to the core like his Scotch-Irish ancestors, and he constantly struggled to overcome that lowly status, which was looked down upon by the upper-class elites on both sides of the Atlantic. In own words in regard to the Creek War in which he compiled an undistinguished record while having gone to war twice despite the strong protests from his wife about leaving the farm and work to be undone, Crockett admitted that he was nothing more than "just a poor soldier." And he was still nothing more than a poor soldier when he served in the Alamo's doomed defense.

Even more ironic, David went to his death without hesitation by following his own much-publicized motto that was well-known to his followers across the United States: "Be always sure you are right, and then go ahead!" But Crockett had been terribly wrong about what he eventually found deep in the heart of Texas, because of the complexities and contradictions of the Texas Revolution of which he was not fully aware, when he first enlisted not only after entering onto Texas soil.

In consequence, the popular Tennessean threw his life away at age 49 in the ill-fated defense of an indefensible old Spanish mission, whose defense had been doomed from the beginning and long before Santa Anna's arrival on ill-fated February 23. In this case, Crockett made a fatal mistake in boldly going ahead too far and too boldly in a determined bid to fulfill his ambitions while risking too much, because he hoped and prayed that he could resurrect his fortunes and overall image in Texas: a Faustian Bargain that cost him his life for no gain at the Alamo.

Tragic, but Heroic Ending

Given all of the best available evidence, especially multiple accounts of the fighting at the Alamo from the words of one of the few noncombatant survivors--Travis' slave Joe who was age 21 and born in Alabama--, which were published and republished in newspapers across the United States, these survivors, including Susanna Dickinson, never mentioned or even hinted at a capture or execution of Crockett as alleged.

Instead, the relatively few civilian survivors of the Alamo revealed that he went down fighting with other garrison members in the heat of battle. In this sense, David Crockett's death was basically an undistinguished demise, but heroic, and little different from the other men who he fought beside to the last.

In the end, he simply died like of other garrison members while facing impossible odds in a doomed defensive position that was indefensible. Crockett succumbed in heroic fashion while fighting beside his fellow Tennesseans--the company of mounted volunteers who were commanded Ohio-born Captain

William B. Harrison--, whose hopes and dreams died with them.

Crockett's alleged execution on Santa Anna's specific orders could primarily be proven to have been true if verified by a non-Mexican account of an Alamo survivor connected to the garrison, like Joe or Susanna Dickinson or another Alamo survivor, or verified in a Mexican battle report or the Colonel Almonte journal written at the time and not years after the battle like the de la Peña memoir.

But Mexican battle reports that were written not long after the fighting ended on March 6 mentioned nothing of Crockett's alleged execution. Like other Mexican veterans, Sergeant Francisco Becerra, who had been captured at San Jacinto and remained in Texas to live a long life, provided some of the most unreliable accounts of the Alamo and the most fictious accounts of all.

Nevertheless, his words have been early utilized in confidence by Texas historians like John S. Ford, who recorded Becerra's story in 1875 which was nearly 40 years after the Battle of the Alamo, and Reuben M. Potter. This situation existed partly because they had trusted the former Mexican sergeant and believed his stories.

This ex-noncommissioned officer of Santa Anna's Army of Operations provided ridiculous accounts about not only Crockett's death by execution, but also that of Travis' death by execution. Of course, Joe's numerous accounts have told a far different story of Travis' death at the 3-gun battery that bolstered the north wall, and Travis was one of the first to fall in the battle that began with the north wall's defense.

And some evidence has indicated that Crockett was also one of the first to fall instead of at the battle's end, as alleged by Becerra, the former sergeant, in his "yarn" and other Mexican accounts. Becerra provided the best known account of Travis' alleged execution when taken prisoner along with Crockett. But in fact, neither execution of Travis or Crockett occurred at all.

However, the ex-sergeant later admitted that he could not recognize either Crockett or Travis just like other soldados, which has additionally undermined his fanciful stories that were true Texas tall tales. At least Becerra was honest in this regard, because no one in the Mexican Army, including Santa Anna, could have possibly recognized Crockett at the time of the battle.

Quite simply and as mentioned, Mexican soldiers, including Santa Anna, on the early morning of March 6, did not know anything about Crockett and what he looked like. Becerra's fabrication of outlandish Alamo stories was only symbolic of the general unreliability of Mexican accounts written down years after the battle, as in the case of the de la Peña memoir, with its dubious provenance, and numerous other Mexican accounts, which are more distinguished by gossip, rumor, and the rewriting from previous printed sources, including newspapers, and folklore than historical facts.

And significantly, Mexican soldier diaries, like that of Colonel Almonte, and letters written at the time mentioned nothing about Crockett's execution, just like the reports of Mexican generals, including Santa Anna, who wrote nothing about it. But as noted Santa Anna mentioned viewing the bodies of Crockett, Travis, and Bowie, after requesting the mayor of San Antonio de Béxar —Francisco Antonio Ruiz—to show him the bloody remains of the Alamo's three primary leaders.

All the best evidence has indicated that Santa Anna never knew anything about Crockett or his fame, until he was shown the Tennessean's body by Ruiz, after the generalissimo had asked him to do so. If Crockett's fame had spread to the Mexican Army, then Santa Anna would have known something about him, and Colonel Almonte, if he knew what Crockett looked like which was a possibility since he had lived in the United States, could have pointed the Tennessean's body to the generalissimo, but such was not the case.

Even more, Seguín's two cavalrymen (Andres Barcena and Anselma Bergeras, who had gathered information, including about the demise of Alamo leaders, from Tejanos and Mexicans in San Antonio immediately after the battle, almost certainly would have informed General Sam Houston at Goliad on March 11, 1836, if Crockett had been killed by execution (sensational news indeed), since he was considered a leader at the Alamo, although just a "high private," in his own modest words.

Again, despite the accurate information and reporting of detailed deaths of leading men at the Alamo such as Travis and Bowie, nothing was said to Houston by the two patriotic Tejanos of Captain Seguín's cavalry command about the alleged Crockett execution when they rode into Gonzales five days after the Alamo's fall.

Later, Mexican accounts, like the memoir of de la Peña who was a sworn enemy of Santa Anna after the war when the generalissimo rightly received almost sole blame from the people of Mexico for having lost Texas, about Crockett's death were written for propaganda purposes from camp gossip when

Santa Anna became the scapegoat, but for good reason, for his disastrous Texas Campaign.

Considerable efforts were made by soldados captured at Santa Anna and survivors, like de la Peña who had expanded his war diary (now not known to exist) into a journal, or more specifically into a postwar memoir, for several years after the Texas Revolution's conclusion, to paint Santa Anna in the most negative light, after he lost the Battle of San Jacinto on April 21, where he was captured by Houston's forces.

After all, the brief words of a single paragraph about Crockett's alleged execution in the de la Peña memoir suddenly surfaced out of nowhere—deep in the heart of Mexico—in 1955, and its timely appearance is unquestionably highly suspicious, like some of its contents, especially the alleged Crockett execution paragraph, to regard to possibly having been written for the express purpose of capitalizing on or to throw water on the Crockett craze that reached a height in 1955.

For ample good reason, this overall situation should have raised a host of serious questions about the authenticity of the de la Peña memoir. For instance, was the Crockett execution entry in the memoir a modern one, which might have been added by a clever forger with money in mind in regard to the inevitable sale of the sizeable document which was only a matter of time, after word spread in the United States about the de la Peña memoir. Likewise, the previous accounts of Crockett's alleged execution from Mexican accounts were hardly credible, until the entire situation changed with the sudden appearance of the de la Peña memoir that bestowed them with credibility and new life in 1975.

Therefore, in conclusion, it is the opinion of this current author that the de la Peña memoir is authentic as a postwar account despite its lack of provenance, but very likely not the brief words of a single paragraph written about Crockett's execution. De la Peña claims to have been present but turned away in disgust at the last moment from the sight of the execution, which is sort of a moral technicality in regard to conveniently providing an excuse to then truthfully admit that he was not actually lying when he penned his Crockett executive narrative after the war, if he did so.

It is the opinion of this current author that the brief Crockett passage was either written by a modern forger or that de la Peña deliberately embellished his manuscript after the war from using readily available—the rumors of Crockett's alleged execution had been published in numerous United States newspapers in the summer of 1836 and in Mexican accounts, and a Mexican author—either de la Peña or a modern one— had access to these postwar accounts or knew of camp gossip about the execution from San Jacinto prisoners. But again, it is the view of this current author that Crockett was not one of the handful of Texas prisoners who had been brought forth after the combat ended to be executed.

Again and as noted, if Crockett had been executed, some well-educated and knowledgeable Mexican officer would have noted it in their letter, diary, or journal—like Colonel Juan Nepomuceno Almonte in his journal, which remained entirely silent about any execution like the colonel, that was captured at San Jacinto--on March 6, and this was simply not the case. All of the Crockett execution tales from Mexican sources surfaced some time after the battle had been fought.

A least one captured Mexican officer (unidentified) and not the assumed Colonel Almonte, who spoke very good English and needed no interpreter and was not confined at the prison camp on Galveston Island, Texas, also mentioned Crockett's execution, after he was taken prisoner at San Jacinto and held in the prison camp on Galveston Island. His story was written in a July 19, 1836 letter by a prison guard at Camp Travis, Sergeant George M. Dolson.

An interpreter for Colonel James Morgan, who operated the prison facility, assigned to the Galveston Island prison camp known as Camp Travis, Sergeant Dolson wrote how the Mexicans had known "the famous Crockett" and identified him, which would have been an impossibility on March 6. Of course, they had very likely only learned of Crockett's presence after his body was pointed out by Mayor Ruiz to Santa Anna.

Again, Mexican soldiers, including Santa Anna until his request was fulfilled on March 6 by the mayor of San Antonio de Béxar, knew nothing of Crockett or what he looked like. As noted, they only later learned from Tejanos, beginning with Mayor Ruiz, of San Antonio de Béxar that Crockett had been present at the Alamo unlike what they had known during the siege of the Alamo and on March 6.

Significantly and as mentioned, the entry in his wartime journal for March 6 and thereafter, Colonel Almonte, or any other Mexican officer for that matter, wrote absolutely nothing about Crockett's capture and execution. And Almonte, a most distinguished officer, was the one man, who had been educated and lived in the United States, in Santa Anna's Army who might have been able to identify Crockett from pictures or his books, if the colonel had seen them when he had lived in the United States—a considerable stretch and flimsy assumption.

However, Almonte failed to mention anything—and this would have been significant news--about the execution of a former United States Congressman, which would have certainly earned an entry in his rather mundane journal. Such omissions from the best primary Mexican sources on March 6 about Crockett and his alleged execution all indicated that while Travis and Bowie were well-known revolutionaries, Crockett was entirely unknown, having only recently arrived in Texas. Travis had been infamous in Mexico City as a leading troublemaker, or "War Hawk," for years and going all the way back to the Anahuac disturbances of 1832, while Crockett was still serving in Congress.

But as mentioned by this time, captured Mexican soldiers, from educated, aristocratic officers to lowly privates of the peasant class, far from home and surrounded by vengeful Texans would say almost anything to their captors in the hope of surviving and eventually getting back to their far-away homes deep inside Mexico, after having been captured at San Jacinto.

As noted, this was comparable and much like the case of Sioux and Cheyenne warriors who said—or indicated by sign language--mostly favorable things, especially in regard to courage, about George Armstrong Custer and his doomed men of five ill-fated companies of the 7th Cavalry during interviews with whites after the defeat in a remote part of the Montana Territory.

Quite simply, the Northern Great Plains warriors said whatever they thought that white interviews wanted to hear, especially about Custer and how he died bravely fighting to the bitter end, after they and their families had become vulnerable after the defeat of the Sioux nation in the years following the Battle of the Little Bighorn on June 25, 1876.

In much the same way, so defeated Mexican prisoners on Galveston Island also told their captors what they thought that they wanted to hear, especially by presenting Santa Anna in the most negative and worst possible light—the epitome of the arch-villain. And to a generation of Americans who knew well of the Crockett's frontier legend that was second to none in folk memory, the story of Santa Anna's alleged execution of one of America's great national celebrities at the Alamo was the most guaranteed way to present Santa Anna as the epitome of evil to prove that the average soldado had been a pawn of the general's bloodlust at the Alamo, when they were ordered to kill every garrison member at the Alamo and all prisoners.

This was certainly a primary motivating factor of de la Peña, who hated of Santa Anna was intense, and this fact was fully reflected numerous times in his memoir, especially the paragraph about Crockett's alleged execution.

In addition and as noted, the alleged dramatic execution of Crockett on Santa Anna's direct orders makes no sense for a wide variety of reasons. First and foremost, Santa Anna most of all needed Crockett as a prisoner for propaganda purposes to prove the extent of outside interference—by early 1836, relatively few Texians were serving in the army's ranks as it was mostly United States volunteers like Crockett—, and there existed no better example of foreign interference than the former Tennessee Congressman. After all, Crockett was one of the best known celebrities in the United States, including on the Atlantic's other side.

Clearly, a captured Crockett would have been Santa Anna's best way to make an excellent case about the widespread extent of illegal military intervention in Texas from the United States that was against United States Neutrality Laws and an entirely illegal activity in the court of world opinion. If Santa Anna could prove his point, then he would be transformed from a villain to the righteous defender of his nation, because of the massive interference in the Texas Revolution from the United States.

For Santa Anna, a captured Crockett—especially since he had been a Congressman from Washington, D.C.--would have bestowed unlimited propaganda value and immense dividends to Santa Anna and the Republic of Mexico, which was beset by internal divisions and financially-strapped unlike the United States. In striking contrast to such an immense propaganda coup, an executed Crockett provided absolutely no advantage whatsoever to the generalissimo or Mexico, who badly needed to win the propaganda war in world public opinion in this conflict against so many newly-arrived American citizens, who were heavily-armed and eager to take Mexico's lands as their own. Another other American prisoner, or an entire group of captives, at the Alamo might have served this purpose, but Crockett was the ideal propaganda piece.

But it is clear that a captured Crockett, the most famous American of his day after President Andrew Jackson, would have provided Santa Anna with enormous assets on multiple levels, and far more than the captured blue banner of the New Orleans Greys that he sent back to Mexico City as significant proof of large-scale outside foreign intervention from the United States, which was not at war with Mexico or vice versa.

For a host of reasons, Crockett's alleged execution was not depicted in film from 1911 and until the year of 2004—nearly a century of a complete absence in the history of filmmaking. But there were other omissions as well when it came to Crockett's death. In 1955, for instance, Walt Disney never depicted the final scene of Crockett's death while fighting to the last breath in a fade-away to the Texas (Lone Star that, of course, was inaccurate) battle-flag waving from the Alamo's battered walls.

Clearly, the different portrayals of Crockett's death in 1911 and 2004 only revealed how America as a nation and American culture had significantly changed long after the Tennessean's final demise in regard to its heroes and their place in cultural memory.

In the end and nearly a half century later, it was left to the 2004 film *The Alamo* to present the most imaginary and fanciful of all Crockett deaths—far more extreme than the popular Hollywood final scenario in multiple films of Crockett attempting to blow up the Alamo's powder magazine, which was nothing more than a dramatic fantasy of the mythical Alamo—by way of a grisly, humbling execution that mocked the frontiersman's reputation as a fighting man: an imaginary scenario that has diminished the real man and what he represented and accomplished in a remarkable life to reduce his lofty hero status that had once dominated the hearts and minds of people across America.

But at least Walt Disney managed to get it right in an amateurish production that looks almost D. W. Griffith-like, but not in racial terms, in its simplistic presentation that was targeted more for children than adults by America's great mythmaker himself. But in regard to Crockett's death, Disney proved not a myth-maker, but actually right on target.

Indeed, the best available primary evidence has revealed that Crockett died fighting gamely—but closer to the battle's beginning rather than at the end and near the church and with some of the men of Captain William B. Harrison's Company of Tennessee Mounted Volunteers, who had initially held their defensive position at the low palisade between the church and the south wall (low barracks), instead of by himself and alone at the battle's conclusion as portrayed by Disney for a suitable dramatic ending. As noted, Mexican accounts about Crockett's alleged execution are too often dominated by hearsay, rumor, gossip, and lack of provenance.

Indeed, unlike America's other great frontiersman of the Ohio Valley, Daniel Boone, the earlier frontier hero of the American people who died of old age on his last western frontier of Missouri, Crockett, the premier frontiersman from the Mississippi Valley, had died in the heat of battle as a military man, a volunteer in the citizen-soldier tradition, beside his countrymen, including quite a few other Scotch-Irish fighters: a tragic fate when he died fighting beside his men from Tennessee, which certainly was the case, given the best available primary evidence.

Based on the most reliable and best evidence, Crockett meet his inevitable fate—ironically a heroic demise in keeping with the American public's image of the mythical Crockett from numerous books, plays, and, of course, the popular *Crockett Almanacs* in a self-fulfilling prophetic end of an immensely popular image that he had long cultivated to the American people—in fighting to the bitter end far from home and family for a cause that he believed was just and righteous.

The words of Joe, William Barret Travis' slave whose numerous newspaper accounts appeared not long after the Alamo's fall, have been too often discounted and ignored, although he was a reliable and accurate witnesses to the events that transpired at the Alamo, in today's fashionable and vogue acceptance of Crockett's alleged execution death.

Most importantly, Joe, who Travis had bought two years before, emphasized in no uncertain terms how: "Crockett died like a hero, surrounded by heaps of the enemy" slain, while battling the flood of soldados, who could not be stopped.

In another account published in newspapers across the United States, Joe emphasized how: "Crockett, the kind hearted [which reflected his Scotch-Irish roots and personal qualities], brave David Crockett, and a few of his devoted friends [of Captain Harrison's Tennessee company of mounted volunteers] who entered the Fort with him, were found lying together, with 24 of the slain enemy around him."

In the end, Crockett died near his assigned defensive position as ordered with his fellow Tennessee boys, and was not later taken as a captive to Santa Anna as a captive to be executed in humiliating fashion away from where some of Captain Harrison's Tennesseans had fallen.

Here, the twisting course of his eventful life, which had begun in East Tennessee in 1786, and his long frontier and political career had finally come full circle at the Alamo. In the Alamo's defense, Crockett truly became the popular folk hero to the American people, which the careful cultivators and promoters of Crockett's frontier image, especially by the Whig Party against President Jackson, had long portrayed with considerable success, but with less foundation in fact: the mythical Crockett.

At the Alamo, Crockett transformed these many layers of fiction, fantasy, and myth about himself into an undeniable reality by dying a hero's death in his last battle. In this way, he truly became an American military hero, which had not become a reality for him during an undistinguished military role in the Creek War during two terms of service.

Ironically, to become a true hero that his publishers, Whig politicians, and others had created for him in shameless fashion for years, Crockett first had to lose his last election in 1835 and then his life in the following year at the Alamo in a tragic rendezvous with an ill-fated destiny that had haunted him for his entire life.

But it had been this ill-fate and hard-luck of a common westerner which had elevated his traditional frontier qualities of feistiness, purity of spirit, self-sufficiency, resourcefulness, and egalitarianism of the common man into the national spotlight, as opposed to the corrupt east coast values and the decadence of the aristocratic urban elite. These eastern qualities of the elite were the antithesis of the self-made western frontier man like Crockett, as he constantly emphasized in his political campaigning and books during a lengthy career as a remarkable common man.

Quite simply, Crockett was seen far and wide in America as a common man of the people, especially the poor farmers and hunters of the western frontier, and he faithfully died as one beside other poor soldiers, who saw Texas as a great opportunity and their last. Therefore, at the Alamo, Crockett created a new man—actually the resurrection of the younger man of the Creek War—who died as a lowly common soldier in battle with a private's rank in the new people's Army of Texas during the struggle for Texas liberty.

Although the loser of two of the four Congressional campaigns which ensured that he was primarily a failed politician on the national stage, and his permanent status of a poor man that he could not overcome no matter how hard he tried or wherever he went, including Texas, Crockett had embarked his greatest gamble when he rode off to Texas and faced his last great trial in life in a battle where the odds were stacked even higher against him, and one that he could never win like in his own personal struggles of a debt-ridden life.

Of course, this cruel fate that awaited him at the old Franciscan mission was one reason why his long-suffering wife Elizabeth had attempted to convince him not to embark upon this dangerous journey into the heart of the unknown and to a strange place that he had never seen before far from his home ground of West Tennessee.

And he lost his greatest and last battles of his life in both the political and military fields in two consecutive years when his luck turned against him with a vengeance. However, in the end, Crockett did indeed go down fighting on the morning of March 6 unlike the current vogue and popular consensus of his final demise, based on rumor, hearsay and highly-dubious Mexican accounts, in America's most unheroic age: that he was taken captive or surrendered, and then was executed on Santa Anna's direct order.

Unfortunately, this alleged Crockett execution scenario has become today's fashionable and politically correct conclusion to a remarkable life and one that has reached new heights in America's most irreligious and anti-hero age during the twenty-first century, as revealed in full in John Lee Hancock's 2004 film *The Alamo* that prominently featured Crockett's alleged execution in an over-the-top and entirely imaginary scene geared toward excessive sensationalism to evidently sell as many tickets as possible.

While a mere handful of prisoners (6 or 7 depending on the Mexican account) were captured at the Alamo on the bloody morning of March 6, 1836 at the battle's end and then were killed by Santa Anna's direct orders because a number of Mexican accounts—all perhaps originally based on a single one derived from camp gossip, hearsay, rumor, or just to malign Santa Anna as much as possible--have coincided and revealed as much, there can be no doubt of the truth in this regard.

But as mentioned, Crockett was <u>not</u> one of these unfortunate men who was captured and executed after the battle had ended. This imagined scenario of Crockett's execution never happened, because he was in fact already dead by this time, having been killed in the heat of battle.

But in fact, if Santa Anna had ordered Crockett's execution because he allegedly knew that it was him (he did not), then he would <u>not</u> have requested the mayor, Francisco Antonio Ruiz, of San Antonio de Bexar, to identify his body almost immediately after the slaughter.

Sadly, the Crockett execution gossip and stories stemmed from the fact that no member of the Alamo garrison survived the bloody battle, and the victors were able to continue to write their accounts, both real and fictional, for years after the battle had been fought to generate a one-sided and biased presentation of the Alamo's story, including Crockett's alleged execution.

As noted, by the time that the executions of a handful of survivors of the Alamo garrison occurred, Crockett was already lying dead near the church and not far from where he had been stationed with the rest of Captain William B. Harrison's small (16 men) band of Tennessee Mounted Volunteers at the low palisade. Susanna Dickinson saw Crockett's body lying near the stone church, and the traumatized widow of Captain Dickinson, like Joe, repeatedly mentioned this fact.

And young Enrique Esparza, only a boy during the Alamo siege and the son of one of the few Tejano defenders, cannoneer Gregorio Esparza who was a member of Captain Juan Nepomuceno Seguín's command, described how Crockett "fell immediately in front of the large double doors [of the church] which he defended with the force [Captain William B. Harrison's Tennessee Mounted Volunteers] that was by his side [and] When he died there was a heap of slain in front and on each side of him."

Like exhibited Crockett's combative ways during the siege and the Creek War, this conclusion by reliable eyewitnesses of what actually happened at the Alamo on March 6—and not much later like Mexican accounts, such as the de la Peña memoir--was in agreement with the many newspaper accounts across the United States that emphasized how Crockett died fighting like "a tiger" to the very end.

Such accounts of Crockett's heroic demise in battle were the antithesis of early newspaper articles that detailed the suicide deaths of not only Lieutenant Colonel William Barret Travis, but also Jim Bowie. However, as created by Hollywood, today's common view of Crockett's heroic death in attempting to blow up the Alamo's powder magazine was a myth. As mentioned, that was the mission of Ireland-born Major Robert Evans, age thirty-six and known for his merry spirit and Irish ways, who died in a desperate and futile attempt to blow up the supply of black powder in a back room of the Alamo church.

Once again in regard to the martyred Crockett who went down fighting against impossible odds and with no chance for survival on that awful March morning at the old Spanish mission to fulfill the heroic aspects of his popular image that existed across the United States at the time, Dr. Isaac N. Jones said it best in the end.

In his letter, he emphasized to Crockett's widowed wife, Elizabeth, about the ultimate truth of Crockett's death in the heat of battle, which was a conclusion based upon more primary evidence than camp gossip, rumor, idle hearsay, and dubious Mexican accounts, especially those without proper provenance: "I cannot restrain my American smile at the recollection of the fact that he died as a United States soldier should die, covered with his slain enemy."

About the Author

PHILLIP THOMAS TUCKER, Ph.D., has won international acclaim on both sides of the Atlantic as today's leading "New Look" historian, who has authored a large number of "New Look" books of unique distinction. One of America's most prolific and groundbreaking historians, Tucker has authored nearly 65 highly original books that have revealed long-ignored and silenced chapters of history, while correcting the historical record for the twenty-first century. Tucker's new book, released in November 2019, and entitled *Custer at Gettysburg, A New Look at George Armstrong Custer versus Jeb Stuart in the Battle's Climactic Cavalry Charges*, has presented a more balanced and complete analysis of Custer's overlooked role in the winning of the Battle of Gettysburg on the decisive afternoon of July 3, 1863.

Bibliography

American Statesman, Austin, Texas.

Brands, H. W., *Andrew Jackson, His Life and Times*, (New York: Anchor Books, 2005).

Columbia Observer, Columbia, Tennessee.

Crockett, David, *A Narrative of the Life of David Crockett of the State of Tennessee, Written by Himself*, (Lincoln: University of Nebraska Press, 1987).

Derr, Mark, *The Frontiersman, The Real Life and the Many Legends of Davy Crockett*, (New York: Quill and William Morrow and Company, Inc., 1993).

Enquirer, Richmond, Virginia.

Flores, Richard, *Remembering the Alamo, Memory, Modernity, and the Master Symbol*, (Austin: University of Texas Press, 2002).

Ford, John S., Papers, Archives Division, Texas State Library, Austin, Texas.

Groneman, Bill, *Alamo Defenders, A Genealogy, The People and Their Words*, (Austin: Eakin Press, 1990).

Guerra, Mary Ann Noonan, *Heroes of the Alamo and Goliad, Revolutionaries on the Road to San Jacinto and Texas Independence*, (San Antonio: The Alamo Press, 1987).

Handbook of Texas, Online.

Hardin, Stephen L., *The Alamo 1836, Santa Anna's Texas Campaign,* (Oxford: Osprey Publishing, 2001).

Hickey, Donald R., *Glorious Victory, Andrew Jackson and the Battle of New Orleans*, (Baltimore: John Hopkins University Press, 2015).

Huffines, Alan C., *Blood of Noble Men, The Alamo Siege and Battle*, (Austin: Eakin Press, 1999).

Jackson, Jack, editor, *Almonte's Texas, Juan N. Almonte's 1834 Inspection, Secret Report and Role in the 1836 Campaign*, (Austin: Texas State Historical Association, 2005).

Kennedy, Billy, *The Scots-Irish in the Hills of Tennessee*, (Londonderry: Causeway Press, 1995).

Kilgore, Dan and Crisp, *James E., How Did Davy Die? And Why Do We Care So Much*, (College Station: Texas A&M University Press, 2010).

Lofaro, Michael A., *Davy Crockett, The Man, The Legend, The Legacy, 1786-1986*, (Knoxville: The University of Tennessee Press, 1965).

Long, Jeff, *Duel of Eagles: The Mexico and U.S. Fight for the Alamo*, (New York: William Morrow and Company, 1990).

The Long-Island Star, Brooklyn, New York.

Lord, Walter, *A Time to Stand*, (New York: Pocket Books, 1990).

Maryland Gazette, Annapolis, Maryland.

Memphis Enquirer, Memphis, Tennessee.

Missouri Gazette, St. Louis, Missouri.

New Orleans Advertiser, New Orleans, Louisiana.

New Orleans Commercial Bulletin, New Orleans, Louisiana.

New York Herald, New York, New York.

Perry, Carmen, translator and editor, *With Santa Anna in Texas, A Personal Narrative of the Revolution*, (College Station: Texas A&M University Press, 1975).

Potter, Reuben M., *The Fall of the Alamo*, (1860).

Richmond Whig, Richmond, Virginia.

San Antonio Daily Express, San Antonio, Texas.

San Antonio Express, San Antonio, Texas.

San Antonio Ledger, San Antonio, Texas.

San Antonio Light, San Antonio, Texas.

Santos, Richard G., *Santa Anna's Campaign Against Texas, 1835-1836*, (Waco: Texian Press, 1968).

St. Louis Republican, St. Louis, Missouri.

The Telegraph and Texas Register, Columbia, Texas.

The Texas Republican, Brazoria, Texas.

Tucker, Phillip Thomas, *Exodus from the Alamo, The Anatomy of the Last Stand Myth*, (Havertown: Casemate Publishing, 2011).

Walraven, Bill and Marjorie, *The Magnificent Barbarians: Little Told Tales of the Texas Revolution*, (Eakin Press, 1993).

Winders, Richard Bruce, *Crisis in the Southwest, The United States, Mexico, and the Struggle over Texas*, (Wilmington: SR Books, 2002).

Winders, Richard Bruce, *Sacrificed at the Alamo, Tragedy and Triumph in the Texas Revolution*, (Abilene: State House Press, 2004).

Zaboly, Gary S., *An Altar for Their Sons: The Alamo and the Texas Revolution in Contemporary Newspaper Accounts*, (College Station: State House Press, 2011).

9 781794 874930